D1108083

ANTI
AGENCY

PRAISE FOR THE AUTHOR'S WORK

Real. Raw. Honest. We live in a world flooded with content disguised as perfection. Overly re-touched photos, color-enhanced, manipulated to the point of breaking the realm of reality. And people think this is real. It's not. The path to success for most entrepreneurs is rarely void of pitfalls and Jason brings those front and center, just as he should. The best advice you can get as a burgeoning business owner is "It isn't easy." All the hard truths are in here, and you should know them before you take the leap. It's also filled with positivity and hope, two things you'll absolutely need as an entrepreneur. Buy it. Read it. Apply it.

– JONATHAN HARRIS, CO-FOUNDER, WILD GRAVITY

I feel that this book is a must read for any agency team member, freelancer, or entrepreneur who is looking to disrupt a specific vertical or industry. Jason provides both big picture thinking and tactical information that is critical to building a successful business.

– LELAND DIENO, VICE PRESIDENT, AGENCY MEDIA

Picking who to take guidance from in life is tricky, and that is certainly true in business. To me, I look for a level of innate understanding and aligned philosophies when seeking guidance. After spending time interfacing with Jason and the philosophies presented in *Anti-Agency*, I felt that alignment and understanding. I can identify with Jason because I felt he identified with me. The "keep it simple" approach in *Anti-Agency* will help you understand business in a way that is smart, practical, and effective.

– ZACH ROSENFIELD, CEO, ROSENFIELD MEDIA GROUP

Jason is someone who can see around the corner. I particularly admire his team dynamic and how they promote a culture of positivity. Socialistics is one of our first strategic partners, and I can't wait to see what the future holds.

– AUSTIN ROSENTHAL, CO-FOUNDER, LIONIZE

Jason not only shares his story in a way that is very relatable and will connect with any aspiring or current entrepreneur, but he shares a ton of valuable, actionable information that you can take with you and apply to your own business. He is able to simplify things in a way that make so much sense and really make the process of starting your own agency feel doable. Any new or aspiring agency owner would benefit and learn a lot from this book and hearing about the personal stories and Jason's approach to entrepreneurship will definitely resonate.

– NICOLE HAMZELOO, CEO/FOUNDER, THRIVE COLLECTIVE CO.

Jason Yormark is incredibly talented and dedicated to providing transparency within the marketing industry. His team's collaborative efforts help us on a monthly basis be able to reach our clients and help with that scary topic no one wants to talk about, insurance!

– SARA EANNI, MBA, CIRMS, ASSOCIATE PARTNER, ABI INSURANCE

Jason's approach to solving problems is unique and fun. He and his team at Socialistics really want to see you succeed and genuinely care about building relationships. They are truly a results-driven partner in your corner. I can't wait to work with them again!

– AMBER JACOBS, OWNER, AMBER DESIGN, LLC

Jason Yormark, and his social media company, were such an intricate part of our business model. In working with both Independent Filmmakers and Independent Film Marketing, his team reflected his great values and his vision and brought our social media to new heights. I would work with Jason again.

– JIMMY HORNBEAK, CMO, THE RANCH FILM STUDIOS

Jason's ability to organize and clarify the chaotic ideas I had, and turn them into a solid marketing plan with measurable results allowed me to grow my company. I have been referring Jason for 10 years to other small business owners who can benefit from his expertise.

– JENNIFER CHILDS, OWNER, CFOALC

Reading Jason Yormark's book, *Anti-Agency*, is like having a playbook for those who have a vision, a dream, an epiphany, to make their quest come to fruition. Whether "quashing the status quo", tilting at windmills, or simply knowing that you have an idea that can change the world for the better, this book is for you.

– KEVIN SCUDDER, ATTORNEY, SCLC

ANTI AGENCY

AGENCY

A REALISTIC PATH TO
A $1 000 000 BUSINESS

JASON YORMARK

Throne Publishing Group
1601 E 69th St #306
Sioux Falls, SD 57108
ThronePG.com

CONTENTS

PART 1: LAYING THE *ANTI-AGENCY* FOUNDATION

PART 2: BUILDING AN *ANTI-AGENCY* BUSINESS

PART 3: GROWING YOUR *ANTI-AGENCY* BUSINESS

PART 4: TAKE ACTION

ACKNOWLEDGMENTS

When you run a virtual business, it can sometimes feel as if you're all alone on an island. But I certainly would not have achieved the levels of success I've had without help from some incredible people.

To my past and current team at Socialistics, you are all rock-stars and the engine behind helping us make Socialistics a world-class social media agency. To Joanna, this business does not exist without your tireless commitment and enthusiasm. Thank you for everything you've done and continue to do. To Ashley, thank you for taking the leap of faith with me on day one and helping us build our life of freedom.

To Jason Swenk and the Digital Agency Elite community, you have been invaluable in helping me navigate some difficult decisions and for being the rock I needed to keep me grounded and have the support from like-minded individuals.

To my boys, Jacob and Justin, for having the patience and understanding of the stresses, time, and sacrifices of starting and running a business. I'm proud of the boys you have been and the men you are becoming.

Finally, to the love of my life, my wife, Molly. Your support and encouragement have never gone unnoticed. Despite the uncomfortableness of me doing my own thing (can you blame a gal who's been with the same company for twenty-five-plus years?!), you supported my path. Nothing gives me more joy than to have proven it was the right one and to be able to give back to someone who is so generous with others. Thank you. I love you.

FOREWORD

I've been fired from every job I've ever held. That is not an exaggeration—it's fact. It took me thirty-five years to realize I just can't work for other people. I'm an entrepreneur, and I thrive from the freedom of choosing what I want to do and how I want to do it. It's not an easy path, but it's the path that's right for me. I guess you're reading this book to see if it's the right path for you too.

So, do you have what it takes to be an entrepreneur? It's not for everyone. It's mostly a series of high highs and low lows. But ask any true entrepreneur if they mind the swinging pendulum and the answer is no. In fact, quite the opposite. It's the adrenaline rush that keeps us going.

I am somewhat of an adrenaline junkie. Mostly in the form of extreme sports like racing cars, mountain biking, snowboarding, and skiing. It's about adventure and the unknown. I take risks and push myself. Each time I go out, it's different and exciting. It's exhilarating when I do something daring. I like living on the edge and get a thrill from near misses.

Much like extreme sports, my entrepreneurial journey has been filled with exciting adventures—high highs and low lows. I worked for a huge corporation in 1999, right out of college. But, ultimately, I didn't feel significant in that role. I started creating websites on the side which, at the time, was still a very new thing and everyone needed one. Within six months, I was creating a ton of websites and doing piss-poor at the corporate job. Guess what? Fired.

In what felt like the blink of an eye (but was actually twelve years), I turned that side gig into a digital marketing agency where I was CEO with over 100 employees. We worked with some huge brands like Lotus Cars, LegalZoom, and Hitachi. Talk about high highs, right? But then there was the time we had a negative cash flow and didn't think we were going to make payroll. The lowest of lows.

Don't worry, in the end, I did stick the landing. After growing the agency to eight-figures, we sold it for a profit. I stayed on with the agency for some time until it was sold again and I made my exit.

Then I tried corporate again. I took a position as Chief Innovation Officer and gave it a real shot for about six months. But again, I did not feel significant. No real high highs or low lows, right? For me, I think the difference is having some skin in the game. As an entrepreneur, you're not just an employee, your business is your livelihood. In hindsight, I self-sabotaged that opportunity, and we agreed it was best to part ways. (Translation: fired) However, I walked away having learned two things. First, feeling significant is the key to my professional satisfaction, and second, I'm not cut out to work for other people.

With newfound clarity, I realized what my next move should be—to mentor others who want to achieve the same goals I'd achieved. This fed my desire for both significance and entrepreneurship.

In 2014, I focused on my personal brand and founded JasonSwenk.com, helping digital agency owners grow, scale, and eventually sell their agency. My sole purpose is to create the resources I wish I'd had. As an agency owner, I felt very isolated and alone. I had no one who understood my problems and challenges, and it took me years to create the right systems and processes to grow my agency.

So, while building my personal brand, I developed an online training outlining the framework that took me a decade to build at my agency. I also started one-on-one coaching and a mastermind group of like-minded agency owners. The mastermind is a cross between group coaching with me as well as peer mentorship. I also started creating a ton of content to help agency owners solve the most common challenges they face at different growth stages. I started the Smart Agency podcast, a YouTube channel, and speaking on stages at marketing agency conferences. I started a weekly blog, wrote a book, and now basically do everything I can to share my experience, knowledge, and expertise with the agency owner community.

At the end of the day, entrepreneurship, in the marketing agency industry specifically, is an extreme sport itself. It takes guts, intuition, and thick skin. And like any sport, you need the right gear to be successful. I've made it my mission to provide a safety net and all the supplies agency owners need to be at the top of their game

Speaking of high-caliber entrepreneurial "athletes," Jason Yormark is one of only a few who come to mind. In this book, Jason outlines his journey from Microsoft executive to social media agency owner—the steps he took, the lessons learned, and all the twists and turns along the way.

Was Jason's a smooth journey? Spoiler alert: it never is. I crossed paths with Jason Yormark a few years ago. He had been following my content for quite some time and joined my digital agency owner Facebook community with over 5,000 members. I talk to dozens of agency owners every week and, truthfully, I don't remember every conversation. However, I distinctly remember my first conversation with Jason because he was very candid.

It is our process for new members to apply online. Then, if they meet our criteria, I personally interview them and determine if we're a good fit for each other. Why go through so much trouble? Well, a mastermind can be a total game-changer for its members and, as they say, you're the sum of the fifteen people you spend the most time with. So, we are really selective with who we allow into the group. When it's done well, a good mastermind provides its members with advanced learning as well as relationships and potential partnerships. We want to protect the reputation and effectiveness of the group with a scrupulous selection process. (Pro tip --> You should always pre-qualify your clients and be selective in choosing ones you can successfully help, so you don't waste time or energy on the wrong ones.) But I digress :) Jason made it to the interview stage, and he made the cut. He applied, he met our criteria, and I approved him for mastermind membership. But ...

The only thing was that Jason was still in the beginning stages of starting his agency and, although I offered him a spot in the group, he ultimately made the decision not to join. Surprised? I know I was after I learned his reason. Jason is totally self-aware. He knows what it takes to be successful as a mastermind member. In the end, he felt he wasn't ready to join the group with such little experience. The key in a group like this is to give more than you take; Jason knew that and realized he wasn't in a position to be much of a giver. That is the definition of integrity and I respect that decision immensely.

About a year later, having continued following my content, growing his agency, and becoming an active participant in my Facebook community, he came back and said, "I'm answering questions in the Facebook community. I feel helpful and I think I can do the same in the mastermind community - I'm ready." You know what? He was.

Jason is one of our model mastermind members. He shows up for the other members. He gives more than he takes and, because of that, when he has a need, others are very generous giving back to him. He learns from others, collaborates with them, and helps when he can. He's vulnerable with the other members which builds trust. And with trust comes more connection and collaboration. It just perpetuates, which in turn propels Jason and his business.

When Jason told me he was writing a book (and consequently having the honor of writing the forward), it came as no surprise at all. As I said, he's a giver with a desire to help others. Writing a book to chronicle his journey and inspire others seems only natural.

My final words are this. Everyone's story is unique, and Jason's is no exception. There is no cookie-cutter approach to starting, growing, and scaling an agency (or any business, for that matter). In fact, nearly everyone I talk to is an accidental agency owner who fell into the opportunity. There's no textbook way to do it, you just learn as you go. Make mistakes and learn from them. Celebrate every win, even the small ones. Take nothing for granted. I'm not going to lie, as I've gotten to know Jason, he's made some decisions I wouldn't have—and I'm sure the reverse is true, too! Even now as we've been working together, Jason asks for advice from the mastermind group and myself. We don't always agree, but, as I said, entrepreneurship takes guts. He's come a long way from the guy I first met to become the guy who is an invaluable mastermind member. That's why everyone's story is unique and exactly why entrepreneurs experience those high highs and low lows they love so much. I would urge you to bear that in mind as you read this book and consider the decisions you're bound to face.

Remember, entrepreneurship is like an extreme sport. So, suit up and have the time of your life!

Jason Swenk
www.jasonswenk.com

PROLOGUE

I love baseball.

When we're young, something typically happens that pushes us down certain paths of passion. For me, that passion was baseball. I grew up in the Chicago suburbs and immediately connected with the magic of Chicago Cubs baseball. At the time, I didn't realize the futility of the organization or the years of disappointment I would suffer through (until 2016!), but it didn't matter. It was magical to me, and I was hooked.

The only thing I loved more than baseball was my mom. She had the difficult task of raising my brother and me as a single parent without our father being part of the picture logistically or financially for most of our youth.

We were poor, but I didn't know it. Although we didn't have much, at the time, I felt I had just about everything I needed. We lived in an apartment complex, and most of my youth was spent simply being outside and playing with the neighborhood kids. Back then, that typically involved playing baseball. If you've seen the movie *The Sandlot*, it's very much the same, albeit 80s style. Just about every day, we would convene in the middle of the complex in a field, pick our teams, and play ball. It was heaven, and it was enough.

That was, until I wanted to play little league baseball. Mom couldn't afford it. She worked relentless hours just to put food on the table. So, the money to pay for the fees, equipment, and uniform wasn't there. Nor was the time to shuttle me to and from practices and games. I was heartbroken. For a few years, I didn't understand why I couldn't have this one thing I wanted so badly. I'm sure that, as a young kid, I didn't make it easy on my mom or truly understand the reality of our world at the time. I do now, and I think about it often.

On my twelfth birthday, my mom handed me an envelope—my gift. Really?! An envelope? What kid would get excited about an envelope as a birthday gift? I was about to find out pretty quickly. As I read through the letter contained in the envelope, tears flowed down my face and excitement coursed through me. Little did I know that my mom had been working her tail off to give me baseball, to find a way to pay for it and get me to and from it. I'll never forget that day. I was young and so caught up in the moment that I didn't realize the sacrifices my mom was making to allow this to happen.

I'm not even sure whether she knew the full impact this decision would have on my life.

In the summer of 1986, I stepped into the batter's box for my first Little League at-bat. Mom was in the stands, grinning from ear to ear. I was overwhelmed, inexperienced, and in over my head. But it didn't matter because I was playing baseball! For real. The days of backyard baseball would pale in comparison to the real thing, and it was time to see if any of it could pay off. While I can't remember exactly how many pitches I saw in that first at-bat, the only pitch that mattered was the one I hit for a home run—in my first Little League at-bat! The only one I would ever hit.

I never stop thinking about the sacrifices my mom made to give me baseball. I would end up playing every year, and I'm pretty sure she was at every game. Sadly, she's no longer with us, but baseball is. I still play, certainly for my love of the game, but also, I think, because it remains a connection to my mom. Every time I hit a double in the gap, round first base, and trot into second, I reflect on my mom and the gift of baseball she gave me so many years ago. And I'm still looking for that next home run.

I share this story because I believe it is a foundational element of who I am and part of my DNA in helping me build and run my agency. I never truly believed I had what it took to build a million-dollar agency, but little did I know, I always did. My journey to get there, however, was much different than most, filled with failures, learnings, and strategies that these days are often an afterthought.

I couldn't be prouder of what we've built, and this book is a love letter to everything we've accomplished. More importantly, it a story that I hope will help others in their journey to building an agency or digital business fueled by compassion, generosity, and authenticity. The *Anti-Agency*.

Thanks, Mom.

INTRODUCTION

I never fit into Corporate America. I was always a square peg in a round hole. But running my own business? No way. That never seemed real to me. Never seemed like a viable option. Especially early on, as I had racked up plenty of college loan debt, had bills to pay, etc. No, I needed a nine-to-fiver, a steady paycheck, benefits, the whole nine yards. I felt it was the only practical course. So, like most people, I followed the path of least resistance right out of the gate.

Job after job ensued. Being a marketer didn't help. Marketers a dime a dozen, right? Well, not really, but that's typically the consensus, and I suffered through my fair share of layoffs, leadership changes, firings, and the occasional market crash. Marketing is usually the first thing to go when that happens. But I continued to trudge along, taking on roles that never really scratched that deep down entrepreneurial itch. I felt frustrated in most of my roles. Ineffective leadership, downright awful managers, unnecessary meeting after meeting. Sound familiar? Have you ever sat in a meeting designed to discuss another meeting? Yea, plenty of those. Sitting in your car for multiple hours a day just to get back and forth to those jobs? When is somebody going to finally invent those damn flying cars?

I played the game for more than twenty years. It took me that long to finally figure out my true calling. That may sound pretty depressing. Trust me, it isn't. Everyone's journey is different. For every guy or gal that figured it out in their early twenties, there's someone who didn't until their forties … or even later. Entrepreneurship isn't a one-size-fits-all proposition. There are many ways to get there. So, if you're stuck in the rut, trust me, there's still time and a path for you.

Does this resonate with you? Are you going through the motions in your job? Do you know intrinsically that you are wired to do your own thing? Then this book is for you. It is a love letter to all the closet entrepreneurs who have yet to pull the trigger, and trust me, I know how hard that can be for most of us.

September 1, 2019. That was my entrepreneurial birthday. That was the day I turned my back on traditional Corporate America and never gave it a second thought. Despite big aspirations with my prior job, like so many others, it fell flat for too many reasons to list in this book. But, luckily for me, I had something in the works that would finally allow me to break from my corporate chains freely and confidently. (More on that later.)

That leap of faith, and everything that has happened with my business since, is detailed in this book. We've done it differently, and I wanted to document and showcase everything that has allowed us to build a million-dollar business from zero. We've gotten as many things wrong as we have right but have learned so much along the way that I felt compelled to share our story with the world. If even one chapter helps push someone else out of the rat race and into the realm of freedom, then the efforts of putting these words on paper will have been worth it.

And that's a word I want to sink in for you now and throughout this book ... FREEDOM. Nothing is more powerful than having control over your life. Your *entire* life. No more being chained to a desk. No more wasting time sitting in traffic every day. I literally have an extra day per week not doing that! The world is changing rapidly, and owning and running a remote-based business is and will be the new norm. It's time for you to be in charge, personally and professionally. Time is just as valuable as money—and believe me when I say that you can have both. There's nothing all that special about me. Now, my team will argue that point, and you'll get perspectives from two of them—Joanna and Ashley—throughout this book. But before you dig in, to help drive home what we've built, let me share some comments from Joanna, our Director of Client Services, one of our first team members:

> *What comes to mind when you hear "agency life"? I'll tell you what I think of. Unreasonable clients, unreasonable requests, long hours often, short hours never, tears, beers, roller coaster office mood, frantic lay-offs, and frantic hires. It's just how agency life is, they say. Well, not if you're Jason Yormark.*
>
> *I started working with Jason, owner of Socialistics, in November of 2019. We are quashing the status quo in a world where an agency's success is often measured by how frantically its people are working. At Socialistics, if a client relationship isn't fruitful for one or both parties, we part ways amicably and respectfully. There are no lock-in contracts, for both of our sakes. Respect for employees and clients AND from employees and clients is the number one priority. The culture isn't free beers at three on a Friday, it is unwavering support from the whole team when life*

happens. We do not clock in and clock out. We're not warm bodies in seats. We get our work done and delivered well and on time.

When there are ups and downs, we respect and support each other. The "office mood" is consistently positive. There is no finger-pointing when something goes wrong. We are a team of humans who help each other learn and grow. There is a lot of finger-pointing when something goes right. The team is recognized, and work is specifically called into the spotlight. We do not churn and burn through employees, and we do not churn and burn through clients.

If you want a standard agency to do a standard job, you've got your pick of the litter. If you want an agency to do an outstanding job because they're an outstanding agency through and through, choose Socialistics.

-Joanna

Joanna and the other team members that have come along on this journey have helped redefine what a marketing agency is, and because of it, we've built a hugely successful business that has allowed us all to live a life of prosperity and freedom. This book might not be your cup of tea, and you might eye roll here and there on some of the concepts we've put into play, but I promise that, if you give it a read, you'll be more convinced and motivated than ever that your time to take the leap is in your near future. And if you've already taken the leap, hopefully you'll find some of our ideas helpful in your continued journey.

I'm just a regular guy that figured out a path. And this book is designed to help you finish carving out yours. Thank you for coming this far, and I hope it helps you build your own *Anti-Agency* Business!

PART 1

LAYING THE
ANTI-AGENCY
FOUNDATION

CHAPTER ONE

YOU HAVE TO FAIL BEFORE YOU FLY

The Big Idea: On your journey toward entrepreneurship, failure and false starts often come before success.

....

They say hindsight is always 20/20. If I could go back in time and advise my younger self on a career path, I wonder what I would tell him. Haircare aside, I almost always think I would choose something other than marketing. When I look at my career, I could stress that I had too many stops along the way ... some of my own doing, some not.

Now, however, I can see how everything I experienced led me to where I am today—running a busy, successful million-dollar agency. From this vantage point, I learned several lessons that may act as signposts you can follow in your journey.

You know what is really hard for me? Talking about myself. I'm terrible at it. To a fault. This was going to be a very different book until my team stepped in and practically demanded I take an alternate route and not write just another how-to marketing book. They were right. So, take a deep breath and follow me on my own personal journey to what led me to where I am today. While your path may be vastly different, I want to provide the context for what experiences (good and bad) contributed to getting me to where I always wanted to be.

A COLLEGE EDUCATION MAY (OR MAY NOT) BE FOR YOU

School was something I had to push myself to do well in. And, admittedly, I didn't push very hard. Just enough to graduate. I didn't take took schoolwork as seriously as I should. In my defense, I had to grow up faster than most kids my age, and getting an education wasn't a priority. It never felt as important as the other aspects of my life.

I didn't know what I wanted to do following high school. All my friends were going to college because "that's what you do." So, I decided to go to a public university where most of my friends had enrolled.

I went down a similar path in college as high school, not taking school work seriously. My grades were terrible the first semester, and I was put on academic probation. That was a real wake-up call. It was time to either put up or shut up—succeed or get my ass kicked out. I enjoyed college socially, making many new friends. It was an adventure being on my own, going somewhere different, charting my own path. The threat of that being taken away frightened the hell out of me. Probation was the catalyst I needed to apply myself.

Looking back, I realize the reason for my apathy was that most of the classed didn't relate to what I wanted to do. Only later, when I got into the classes associated with my interests—courses like broadcasting and marketing—did I excel. I pursued a degree in communications as a result.

Getting a college education forced me to grow up and be more responsible. It gave me the life experiences I needed to start down a career path. I'm not suggesting that a degree is necessary for everyone wanting to start their own business. Many entrepreneurs are successful without it. Look at Bill Gates. He left Harvard in 1975 to found Microsoft. Steve Jobs dropped out of Reed College in Oregon after a single semester. (I guess you could say he was sort of successful.) And what about Mark Zuckerberg? At the end of the 2005 fall semester, he told *The Harvard Crimson*, the school newspaper, "I'm not coming back."

Also, you have to ask if getting buried in thousands of dollars of student loan debt is worth it, especially when so much opportunity to start your own business is available at any age or education level.

FIND YOUR ENTREPRENEURIAL SPARK

Finding your entrepreneurial spark is critical to success. For me, the spark was lit when, in my sophomore year, I decided to work with a company that hired college students to run painting businesses during the summer.

I wanted to do something big, and making a lot of money was very appealing. It was challenging at first, even overwhelming at times. Hiring college students to paint people's homes is a stress-filled, anxiety-ridden enterprise, and it didn't come without failure. Ultimately, however, I ended up being one of the more successful individuals in the company.

The first summer, I did more business in the area than anyone had ever done. That enabled me to make more money than I ever had, which I used to buy a car. The following summer, I nearly doubled the business and my income as a result.

I learned a bigger lesson from that experience than any in college—when I am thrust into an entrepreneurial environment, I do well. Really well. Better than most, if those two summers are any indication. Not only was my entrepreneurial "spark" lit … it was bursting into flame!

EXPECT FRUSTRATION FROM LACK OF CONTROL

Being in control of my fate was a powerful motivator. I never enjoyed having a manager or boss. (I wanted to be my own boss!) Whenever I've been in settings where I am in charge, I thrive.

The desire for leadership has long been a driving force in my personal and professional life. (If you're an entrepreneur, it will be for you, too.) Even at a young age, I would take lead roles in school musicals and plays. As I grew in my career, I sought out speaking opportunities at conferences. I was comfortable being in front of people, the center of attention. There was something very satisfying about it.

Although I didn't realize it at the time, what I was doing was what I was meant to do. In the cases where I was given leadership opportunities, I responded positively. But, once I graduated college, I thought I should get a "real" nine-to-five job because, again, "that's what you do." I didn't really grow up in a family environment that provided any guidance or examples of an entrepreneurial path. Even though I had gotten a taste of it during my college summers, it still didn't seem like a feasible option post-school. I had bills, school loans, and ultimately had to take the path of least resistance … a "real" job.

I graduated college in 1997 and made several questionable decisions. I took a managerial job in a video store in my college town because I was serious about a girlfriend who lived there. The town didn't really offer any opportunities that aligned to my degree, so I took what I could get. After six months, I felt I was selling myself short and moved back to Chicago to regain my momentum in a field that fit my skillset and education.

LEAPFROGGING FROM JOB TO JOB

My early career was a series of leapfrogs from one job to another. The tension between "that's what you do" versus "strike out on my own" was always there. Out of fear, I gave way to the stability that working for a company offered instead of taking on the entrepreneurship challenge. I was like a pendulum swinging back and forth in constant motion, never finding a happy medium.

The endless "Groundhog Day" cycle of going from job to job resulted from my desire for leadership trying to exert itself. It always pushed against the limits imposed by an employee role. I never felt comfortable in controlled environments where I was unable to do what I wanted—take the chances, risks that can usually lead to bigger things.

I continued doing side jobs and started coaching girls' volleyball at a local high school. I was good at it, and the team had an incredible season. I decided I was so good at coaching that I should become a teacher, so I went back to college to earn a master's degree. (Mind you, this coming from the guy who hated school.) I continued coaching and doing side jobs designing websites and was promoted to varsity coach. Toward the end of my master's program, I had to student teach. I realized quickly that coaching and teaching were two very different disciplines and that I had made a horrible miscalculation. I loved coaching, but teaching? Not so much. My classroom experiences quickly led me to realize I had made yet another misstep in my career.

MY 'ALMOST' DREAM JOB

I had never really given up on marketing and side gigs, and, because of that, I was able to maintain some very meaningful and ultimately critical connections. Through one of those, I found out that Microsoft was hiring. A colleague asked if I would be interested in applying, and, of course, I said yes. At the time, I would say that Microsoft was on my shortlist of dream jobs, so I started the interview process. They moved me along the recruiting path and flew me to Seattle. Ultimately, I landed the job as a search account manager, onboarding small-to-medium businesses to Microsoft's search platform. It meant moving to Seattle, but that was a no-brainer. It was a celebrity opportunity I was excited to take.

I was one of Microsoft's first hires for their advertising group, one of three team members. My ascent was quick, and I became a lead, managing the team. As the team grew, I took on recruiting, interviewing, and hiring responsibilities. It was a huge learning opportunity, both from the training aspect and the experience of interviewing hundreds of people from all over the world. Eventually, I managed a team of thirty-five people and was on a "rockstar" path. This was the role I was cut out for, my moment to take off. Then my world suddenly came crashing down when, in October of 2006, my mom had a brain aneurysm and was in a coma.

I flew back to Chicago. Sadly, my mother never came out of the coma and passed away two days later. I was destroyed. I went down a dark tunnel. I felt responsible. My wife and I had two children by that time, and they were mom's world. Even though she had encouraged me to move because of the job opportunity, it meant taking her grandkids away.

I had been determined to make enough money to move her to Seattle, but that never happened, and I carried that guilt for a long time. I struggled once I

Don't discount any of the education, jobs, or "missteps" you take throughout your career. They all matter and will play a part in your entrepreneurial journey. Although I didn't ultimately become a teacher, what I learned along the way was pivotal in my ability to teach and educate later in my career.

returned to work and told my boss I couldn't continue to manage such a large team. She transitioned me into a role with no management responsibilities.

Over time, I rebounded and moved to the Microsoft Community team. I started doing a lot with social media and video. I did great work and even won awards. I was, once again, on an upward trajectory—or so I thought. In 2009, Microsoft did something it had never done in the company's history, laid off five thousand people. My job was on the "outsourceable" list. I was just a number on a spreadsheet. Once again, the stability I thought a job would provide wasn't there.

One of the best things you can do for your career and/ or entrepreneurial journey is to prioritize your personal brand. No matter what you end up doing, investing time and effort into promoting yourself through your own website/ blog is invaluable. Run, don't walk, and get something out there that can showcase what makes you ... you.

The day after I was laid off, I wrote a blog post about being let go. CNET picked it up. The following day, I had ten thousand people on my personal blog. That was the wakeup call I needed. A kick in the ass to get my personal brand cleaned up and leverage this new attention. It was a turning point in my professional life and started the blogging and social media work that would eventually lay the foundation for my success.

Despite the setback, I was determined to get rehired by Microsoft. I had my personal website lying around collecting dust and took time to invest in building my personal brand. I grew a large social media following and began speaking at conferences. Within six months, they hired me back based on my brand-building efforts.

I was placed in a contract role launching social media for the last physical version of Microsoft's Office product for Mac. My success in that role led to me being rehired full-time as the Senior Community Manager for Microsoft Office. Within a month, I realized I had made a mistake. I had tunnel vision about getting back to Microsoft and didn't take the right job or the right team. It was not the same environment as before. A set of "right time, right place" circumstances had enabled me to land the previous job, but that wasn't the case this time.

About eight months later, I left and took a job with a PR firm in a leadership role to build a social media team. I grew that part of the business and experienced great success, but the firm replaced me with someone from a competitor who could bring their client portfolio in exchange for my job. Just another example of not being in control of your own fate.

Still, that entrepreneurial spark kept bursting into flame, and, after a couple of years, I started my own agency. I built it up and had some good success, but my decisions around the types of clients we took on did not scale. I was also going through a divorce at the time, and the business wasn't providing enough income to cover spousal and child support.

I took a job at another agency, which put me in a good place financially, and I thought I could keep my business going on the side. But leading a team of fifteen people at the other agency made it impossible, and my little agency went away. The career pendulum continued to swing, however, and I took a job with a fitness manufacturing company.

This job went very well. I built a successful team, had great results, was happy, loved the people I worked with, and started to think I may have found my forever job. My manager was a true mentor, someone I respected and learned from. But when he moved on and new leadership came in, things fell apart; they wanted to do things differently. I learned another valuable lesson—even when you are a rock-star employee(s), there are still no guarantees.

That's when I launched the Socialistics brand. I didn't know if I could do it full-time, but I created it as a safety net while looking for a job. I looked into a couple—an agency job that paid well but had a long commute and a remote position with a Chicago-based company where I would be vice president of marketing. Neither worked out. The call to entrepreneurship was ringing in my ears louder than ever.

TAKE THE ENTREPRENEURIAL LEAP

If you want to be an entrepreneur, at some point you're going to have to swallow hard, slap yourself in the face a couple of times, and, as Nike says, "Just do it."

Eventually, I came to that point where I had a belly full of "leapfrogging" and was ready to take one more jump—the final one, I hoped—and go with Socialistics full-time. Within a couple of months, I came to terms with the number one thing that had been holding me back: fear. As soon as I realized the stability that I was always looking for was right in front of me the entire time—working for myself, controlling my own fate—the fear melted away, and I took off.

I wasn't the only person to take the leap. Ashley, my first employee, was someone I had worked with previously. Despite the uncertainty starting a new business brings, she joined me wholeheartedly.

"I was the first hire even before Socialistics was founded. Jason and I worked together at another company where we learned that we worked together very well. When the ship started sinking at the other job, I quit without knowing when the next paycheck was going to come to help him relaunch the company. I had full faith in Jason's vision, and I knew we would be fine. Within two years, we went from two clients to close to becoming a million-dollar agency." ~ Ashley, Director of Business Development

OTHER ENTREPRENEURIAL LESSONS LEARNED

As important as those lessons are, they certainly were not the only ones I learned along the way. Here are some others that may benefit you on your journey.

EMBRACE WHO YOU ARE

I am a "breadth" guy, meaning I don't always like doing the same thing. That's something I was afraid to admit for a long time but eventually came to accept. The truth is, there is as much value in being good at juggling many things as there is at being really good at just a few. You're going to have to accept your limitations and learn to work with your strengths while finding ways to offset your weaknesses. Don't shy away from what makes you who you are. Everybody is good at certain things and not so good at others.

SEEK OUT MENTORS

When you're younger, you need guidance and mentorship. For the most part, I never had mentors and had to figure things out on my own, which is why it took me longer to get where I am than it should have. Find people you respect who have a vested interest in helping you improve. (I discuss mentorship in-depth in chapter seven.)

DON'T BE AFRAID TO TAKE RISKS

Entrepreneurship is not for the faint of heart. It is a pothole-filled path best-suited to the risk-taker. You will fail, and there's nothing wrong with that. It's okay to make mistakes, so long as you learn from them.

NOT EVERYTHING WILL BE FUN

Not everything you do is going to be fun or enjoyable. Accept the fact that results come from hard work, doing things you may not want to do. Being great at something comes from working through those sorts of things. People who try to skate by as I did are in for a rude awakening.

DON'T GIVE IN TO THE 'THAT'S WHAT YOU DO' MINDSET

Following the crowd kept me from realizing my true potential for many years. It wasn't until I abandoned the mindset of doing something just because everyone else was that I found my true calling.

CHAPTER TWO

THE RUNWAY PLAN: A REALISTIC PATH TO GOING ALL IN FOR THE REST OF US

The Big Idea: Lay a foundation for success before going full time using the Runway Plan.

....

Part of the fear associated with entrepreneurship is the sheer size of the task. Most people don't have investment money or huge savings to use in starting a business. You must assume many risks and do everything yourself, especially at first. And with that responsibility comes uncertainty. Will I be successful? Can I make this business work? What will happen if I don't? How do I overcome the fear? Do I want to expose my family to the struggle and stress?

Those are reasonable concerns and why I encourage entrepreneurs to take a "runway" approach. By that, I mean building a foundation so that you stand a much better chance of succeeding when you do launch full time.

Socialistics lived for a year as a side hustle before it went full time. Having that onramp allowed me to generate momentum so that, when the right time came, I could start more quickly than if I had begun with nothing. I felt it would be more realistic to change course if I jumped on a plane already heading down the runway rather than building one from scratch. I knew I wanted to be my own boss, but I didn't have the start-up capital. If I was going to get to that point, I needed a runway.

This approach won't eliminate all the risks, but it will help you avoid some of them. That's especially true if you're building an agency or digital business that relies on brand recognition and search visibility. It takes time to gain traction.

RUNWAY APPROACH PRINCIPLES

With that in mind, here are ten principles drawn from my experience that you can apply before launching your business full time.

1. DECIDE ON YOUR TIMELINE AND WORK BACKWARD

Step one is to create the timeline for when you want to go full time. Do you want to shoot for a year, two years, three? Don't give yourself too much time, however, or you may delay putting in the effort it will take to make your entrepreneurship dream a reality.

Once you decide, work backward in your planning. Figure out your income goals and how many leads and sales you will need to achieve them. Give yourself a year or two to establish a brand. It will take a year minimum to gain any sort of search visibility and brand recognition.

Take tangible steps early on. Get a business license. Set up a bank account. Register a domain name. You will also need to design a website and create content like blog articles and social media posts. That will help you add value and build an audience so that, when you open the doors, you already have a rich history of helpful, informative content behind your brand.

By the time I took Socialistics full time, I had a website, reams of content, social media, and a few clients along with examples of their work—all the infrastructure I needed. That enabled me to create a sales pipeline. From the get-go, I had a small yet steady stream of organic leads through search and social media from people looking for the services I offered and a modest portfolio of clients I was working with.

Doing the heavy lifting—building the runway—fostered an environment that made it much easier to go into business 100 percent of the way and not look back. I jumped into a thriving business that had a history of work I could build from. It's a lot easier to get more clients when you have some already.

2. CREATE A PROFESSIONAL BRAND IMAGE

Some people say that your company name, tagline, or logo don't matter; I strongly disagree. Having a professional-looking brand image makes a world of difference. For one, it gives you a sense of pride that generates an emotional connection to your business. My excitement over the company name and logo gave me added drive to put in the time and effort to design a first-rate website and create kickass content. That, in turn, helped me get found online, which led to inbound leads and new business.

Currently, we get fifteen to twenty inbound agency leads a month. That didn't happen overnight, of course. It takes persistence and patience to build the kind of traffic that produces those results. Even if you have a full-time job, you can devote time to building a side brand that lays a foundation to make the transition more manageable and less painful. A brand you can be proud of will spur that momentum.

3. DEVELOP A CONTENT PLAN

Creating content is vital if you want to get found online, but it should not happen haphazardly. You need a plan.

The first step is to create a content calendar (sometimes called an editorial calendar). Consider the topics you want to cover and the frequency with which you will produce content. If you're serious about being found online, you should blog at least once per week and post to social media three to five times per week. This level of activity produces search signals that create influence.

The sum of those efforts will deliver results in the form of leads and sales. You can't treat this like a light switch—sometimes on, sometimes off. It takes consistent effort to build a digital presence.

Don't get caught up in the minutiae of social media posting. You may ask yourself what's the point of posting something today. Is anyone really going to see this? It's not about what you do on any given day, but the sum of your efforts over time. Think of your content marketing like fuel in a car. If you don't continuously put it in, the business won't run.

4. MAKE RELEVANT CONNECTIONS

Reach out to like-minded people, organizations, and websites and ask to write a guest post or offer a link to your resources. Actively participate in groups that relate to your industry and service offerings.

Put in the time—an hour or two a day—to generate that kind of momentum. The more time you put into it, the more likely you will reach your goal of going full time sooner. At the very least, you give yourself some cushion in the event you lose your job. If you do this for six to eight months, your outreach will be more well received because you have built a recognizable brand.

Facebook Groups are rising in popularity, and I guarantee there is one, if not many, that relate to your business. Find them, join them, and participate in them. Better yet, consider starting one as a free, value-adding resource to help grow your authority and influence!

5. CONDUCT COMPETITIVE RESEARCH

Get some guidance by seeing what others in your industry are doing and learning from them. Look at those you will be competing against who are doing well and pick up ideas you can replicate. You want to be different, sure, but you don't have to reinvent the wheel completely. A significant percentage of your work won't be that much different than what others are doing. One of the things I did early on was build a spreadsheet of all the social media agencies I could find in the world, allowing me to gather their information and really understand the competitive landscape. This can be an invaluable tool for you, so take the time to put this together to help you learn and adjust your approach.

6. DEFINE YOUR PRODUCT AND SERVICE OFFERINGS

The landscape of digital business is growing every day, and standing out amongst a sea of competition has grown increasingly difficult. If I could go back and do anything differently, I would definitely make sure our business catered to a more specific audience or demographic. Better to be a big fish in a small pond than the other way around. Whatever business or agency you are considering starting (or even if you're in the early stages), start thinking ASAP about what specific vertical, industry, or customer type you can narrow your focus around. The more narrowly you can define your product and service offerings, whether by industry or type of offering, the higher your likelihood of success. We chose to position ourselves horizontally as a B2B social media marketing agency rather than vertically as a generalist agency offering everything. While I would have taken it a step further and chosen a specific vertical, you can't be all things to all people. It's better to specialize and meet a specific need. Your path to success will be a hell of a lot easier if you do, especially if you consider the amount of competition in high-volume industries.

7. ESTABLISH YOUR CORE VALUES

The real currency in business is trust. People do business with those they trust (and like). There are plenty of successful, talented businesses in the world to choose from, and if you try to compete on price or other "me too" propositions, you are going to lose. Building a successful business is about building trust with your customers and clients. And your core values are the foundation to building that trust.

"We're the anti-agency because everyone has a voice on the types of clients we want, how the agency should be run. It comes down to core values—how we treat each other and the types of clients we bring on board." ~ Ashley

Your core values are essential for a couple of reasons. First, they will help you land business. Prospective clients are more likely to trust you if they know who you are and what you stand for. Second, they come into play when you start building a team. You want to find people who embrace your values, so use your core values to attract the right candidates and filter out the rest. Determining your values should not be difficult so long as they represent what's important to you authentically and transparently. You can't "manufacture" them. Establish them, flesh them out, and put them center stage. And most importantly, live them and foster them throughout your business and the people you bring on board.

8. BE CERTAIN OF YOUR INTENT

The world of virtual assistants is exploding, and they can be an extremely affordable and helpful way to keep the lights on your growing brand if you are still working full time. Do a web search for "virtual assistants" and you will see there is no shortage of companies that can help you find someone to fill whatever gaps you have.

You must know you're going to do this. It has to be an inevitability, not "if" but "when." I do not recommend anyone go down this path without feeling 100 percent certain you have the entrepreneurial spirit in you. If you are not sure, you won't put in the time and effort or have the motivation, determination, and drive to build the runway. Many times, earlier in my life, I thought I was ready to take the leap, but I wasn't. But that didn't mean I wasn't ready to at least get the ball rolling. Make sure you have the right mindset about what is in store for you before you set things in motion.

9. PRACTICE SELF-DISCIPLINE

Working full-time and building a runway takes discipline. Treat the side hustle like it's a part-time job. It may not be your primary source of income—or none at first—but you must still make time for it, whether that means waking up early and putting in an hour or two before work or doing it at night when everyone else has gone to bed. Carve out time every day to contribute to the effort if you want to be successful.

10. SET REALISTIC EXPECTATIONS

You may not make money for a while. In fact, you may want to offer your services for free to build a portfolio. Entice people to work with you, as there is great value in social proof. Working for free or at a discount helps you build a portfolio and get testimonials. If your business is product based, give away some items for free or at a steep discount at first in exchange for reviews, case studies, and testimonials. You need to get people talking favorably about your products and services, and while that may cost you up front, what you gain in return is well worth the investment.

RUNWAY APPROACH BENEFITS

There are several benefits you can experience by taking the runway approach:

INCREASE CONFIDENCE AND REDUCE FEAR

My fear and uncertainty were lessened by the fact that I was already walking into something in motion. The mind can play tricks on you, and you must get past that. This approach increases confidence because it puts you in a place that makes for an easier transition.

GAIN SUPPORT FROM YOUR INNER CIRCLE

It helps to have buy-in from family and friends when you start a business. People you are supporting need to believe in what you're doing, or it will be an additional weight on your shoulders you don't need to carry. My wife was uncomfortable with the thought of me stepping out on my own at first, but I turned that around quickly by building success early on. As I had a plan, things already in motion, and had invested a lot of time in the business and transition, her opinion and support increased tenfold as opposed to starting from scratch out of the gate. Having her and my family's support and confidence made a huge difference in my mental health and ability to move forward confidently.

MITIGATE RISK

I have talked at length about how using a runway approach enables you to mitigate risk, even if you can't remove it altogether. Hopefully, you can put the money you're earning aside to build a business nest egg to give you a cushion when you do take the leap.

PROVIDE PROOF OF CONCEPT

Starting as a side business allows you to iron out the kinks and learn what works and what doesn't. It provides the opportunity to take risks you couldn't otherwise when more is on the line. You may learn that your initial ideas don't work, but now you have the time to make the necessary adjustments in a more risk-free environment, since you are not relying as heavily on your new business yet.

RUNWAY APPROACH CHALLENGES

Believe me, starting a business isn't all fun and games, even if you use the runway approach. Challenges exist as well.

REQUIRES INVESTMENT

Most people don't have much money to pour into a new venture, but you can't go into this without investing some. If possible, put a few thousand dollars away to outsource tasks you are not well suited for, build the basic infrastructure, and cover ongoing expenses. If you are not ready to take that kind of risk, the entrepreneurial life may not be for you. Nothing good comes free.

FEAR OF CUTTING THE CORD

Cutting the cord with a job that provides a stable income and benefits like health care and retirement, isn't for the faint of heart. That's where self-confidence in your abilities factors in, and it is yet another reason to pave a runway first. You can't allow fear to cripple you or your business. The minute I was able to conquer that fear and remove it from my psyche, my business took off.

LACK OF KNOWLEDGE AND EXPERIENCE

You may be starting a business with little knowledge or experience. Don't let either of those be roadblocks. If you're convinced it's the right step, you can overcome both. Self-educate, be passionate, and attack your shortcomings. You can't know or be everything, so find the help and resources to fill the gap.

WITHOUT A RUNWAY, YOU CAN'T FLY

Let's be honest, most people in the world don't have the resources or connections to allow them to start a business comfortably. If you're like me, you've got to grind, be resourceful, and come up with creative ways to make it your reality. That is why the runway approach is so important to folks like us. It buys you time. Time to work things out, learn, test, grow, and build confidence in a business that can, eventually, be a landing spot when the time is right for you.

Progress not perfection … one of my favorite sayings. Don't worry about being perfect. Take the first step and start working toward building something. Make every day count, and, like me, you'll eventually break free from your corporate stranglehold!

CHAPTER THREE

YOUR STORY IS YOUR DIFFERENTIATOR

The Big Idea: Telling an authentic story is the best way to earn a prospect's trust and win their business.

....

It's a given that people do business with those they like and trust. It's also a given that marketing services are a commodity and incredibly oversaturated. If you don't have a unique angle or story, you will get buried right out of the gate. On the other hand, telling your story authentically is the best way to earn a prospect's trust and win their business.

TRUST AND LIKEABILITY: THE REAL BUSINESS CURRENCY

For most digital businesses, the real currency today is trust and likeability. That may be less true for point-and-click product businesses—in those cases, trust is not as important as price and how quickly you can get it—but it is absolutely the case for higher-ticket items or relationship-based, service-oriented businesses. People must like and trust you before they will do business with you.

For service-based businesses, the world is in a much different place. We were already on a path to a more digital-centric world, but the coronavirus pandemic of 2020 added fuel to the digital fire. More and more, people spent their time and money online versus offline, forever changing the business landscape. The lasting effects are still happening, so it's critical for any business to develop strategies around building trust.

Like love, trust comes at different levels, on a scale. How much does someone like and trust you? In many cases, it takes quite a bit to win someone over and turn them from casual observer to buyer. Trust is the ultimate decision driver. The bigger question is how you go about building it.

We have had several opportunities to work with companies that had been wronged by other agencies and that needed to rebuild trust personally and within the agency relationship. Almost half of our sales process typically involves education, or, at the very least, cleaning up the mess left by a previous agency.

In one example, the Air Force came to us with a high level of distrust based on its experience with another agency. Its previous firm was extremely difficult to work with and made it hard to understand the work it did and the subsequent results.

We took time to understand the people and their goals and objectives and to learn why they had been unhappy with the other agency. We got to the root of what they wanted from the relationship: transparency on the work we do, delivering real, measurable results, and making it easy for them to understand how it all comes together.

At the time, one of our differentiators was that we offered month-to-month terms. It sends a message that we believe so strongly in what we do that we don't make you commit to a long-term relationship. However, it puts us in the position of having to earn our clients' trust every month. In this way, we build trust without having to say a word. That was important in this situation because the client needed something to alleviate their built-up distrust with agencies. Giving them a no-risk option allowed us to immediately build a level of trust that helped us win their business. While we don't offer monthly terms on a regular basis any longer, sometimes you must go outside of the box if the situation warrants it. In this case, having the Air Force in our portfolio more than justified the move.

It's like the runway approach I talked about in the previous chapter—planting seeds that will lead to long-term relationships. We spend time with them and have conversations to reinforce who we are and what we do. You must come through and do what you say you will do. Have confidence in your ability to deliver. If we don't feel as if we can deliver or that we are not a good fit, we tell them at the outset and don't pursue the relationship further. That's part of our story.

A client we worked with early on came back to us recently. They weren't ready earlier, and that caught up with them eventually. We parted ways on a good note, however. When the opportunity presented itself again, they returned because they trusted us and are now investing almost double what they spent with us previously as a retainer-based client. Trust and likeability create a lasting effect.

You're going to have some slip-ups in your early days, especially when it comes to choosing who you work with. That's okay. The most important thing is that you learn from these experiences, and, if you do get into business relationships that ultimately go south, that you assess these situations and try to leave on a good note. You never know when good things can ultimately come from these missteps.

THE VALUE OF TELLING AN AUTHENTIC STORY

The million-dollar question is, how do you get prospective customers and clients to like and trust you? You do that through stories.

Now, suppose you have a product or service that competes on price, simply doing what everyone else is doing, offering things that have no weight or significance. In that case, this won't work for you. You don't have an authentic story to tell. New businesses and products are launching every day, and the choices consumers and businesses have are growing exponentially. Having a "me too" product or service is a death sentence.

Many companies say customer service makes them different or their pricing is better. Those aren't stories. Everyone says that. Good customer service and great pricing is not a differentiator, and if you try to lead with either of these, you're going to go out of business fast.

What is your unique value proposition? What makes you different? Why should people care about you? Why do you do what you do? Who are the people behind what you do? Those are the stories you need to be telling.

Pulling back the curtain to provide visibility and insight into who you are creates an environment where people want to do business with you. That is where a lot of companies fail. They don't incorporate stories or narratives into their marketing strategy and how they present themselves. It's a missed opportunity, and your ability to grow is dependent on it. Take some time to research and see what your competitors are doing with their website or social media. Do they blog regularly? Are those blog posts interesting or compelling? Do they incorporate storytelling? How about their social media? Do they post regularly? Is their content even remotely interesting? I'm willing to bet the answer is no to most of those questions for the majority of what you find. And that's good news for you because it means a huge opportunity for you to disrupt.

While throwing money at advertising or PR is a workable strategy, not everyone can do that. Sure, plenty of businesses are fortunate to have access to resources that allow them to get by without telling their story. Instead of that, connect with people to compete with those who don't. You do that by establishing your authentic story. You can't just make things up. Be true to who you are and embrace that.

For as long as I can remember, I have always been the type of person who enjoyed variety in my work. I get bored easily. I'm definitely not the type of guy who can do the same thing every day. For those who do and can pull it off … I'm impressed. Seriously. Because I'm incapable of it.

Early in my career, I perceived this way of working as a weakness and always tried to hide it, especially when it came to interviewing for new roles. Of course, the truth is businesses need people who are great at breadth and depth. Having team members who can do well at juggling a great many things is equally as important as someone who goes deep with a few. The biggest lesson for me in this regard was that it took strength and courage to finally embrace who I truly was and the value I brought to whatever company I was with.

Embrace who you are and what your business is. Don't be something you're not or say what you think people want to hear. It doesn't scale. There's an audience for your story. Don't try to be everything to everybody. Don't worry about offending people. You can't make everyone happy. Be true to who you are, attract the people who want what you offer, and be the best for them.

Don't be overly prescriptive in your marketing either. Use storytelling to create a narrative around why and how you do what you do and provide examples. People are more likely to consume those sorts of things than prescriptive, formulaic content.

Stories are what pull people in and get them interested. Storytelling goes back to the beginning of time, but many companies fail to approach their business in a way where they tell stories. It's a lesson they have yet to learn, which can work to your advantage.

STORIES CAN FIND YOU

Sometimes the best stories find you or happen to you when you least expect them or plan for them. A few years ago, I was invited to participate in a tech TV show in Toronto, Canada, to discuss social media. In the throes of my excitement, focusing mainly on preparing for my appearance, my passport situation became an afterthought.

Unfortunately, I waited until a few days before my trip before realizing I had lost it. Now I was in a bind. Like most people, I turned to Google for a solution, desperately looking for how to get a passport in a day. There wasn't much information available at the time, and it took a ton of piecing things together from different websites to figure out how to pull it off. Luckily, I found my way, and was able to get the passport in time for the trip.

But that's not where my story was found.

I arrived at the airport with a few hours to spare and thought to myself, "I can't be the only person who has gone through this." I figured, why not take what I learned and put together a blog post detailing the specific steps on how to get a passport in a day to help others avoid having to go through what I did. I fired up my laptop, searched "same day passport" keywords, wrote up the blog post "9 Steps to a Same Day Passport," hit publish, jumped on the plane, and didn't give it much thought after the fact.

So, how did this become a story that found me? To this day, that post is the most trafficked one on my personal site (and chances are that it will still be whenever you're reading this). Hundreds of thousands of hits and I'm still getting thank you messages from people whom I've saved in their own passport crises. While I can't say with certainty that it's led to any business, it has brought a tremendous amount of attention to me and my website and helped build an audience … just by taking a situation in my own life and helping others.

Stories surround you every day. Find the challenges and solutions in your life and turn them into stories for your audience. Be helpful. Be entertaining. Provide added value, and you will find a path to a massive uptick in traffic to your website(s).

STORYTELLING DEFINED

Don't merely be prescriptive. Take facets of what you do and why and create a narrative around them. For instance, I wanted to build an "anti-agency" to do things the way I wanted and that I felt was right. That's the world I wanted to live in and create for other entrepreneurs. I wanted my story to feel like a TV show or movie, not just regurgitate what everyone else was saying.

Story needs to be intrinsic. Weave in anecdotes about your business and what you do using blogs, podcasts, social media, and conversations with prospects.

Story can have different faces. It can be your own story or the stories of others, such as your employees or clients. Capturing client stories in the form of case studies is a great way to garner attention from prospects. Turn their experience with your company into stories—how you landed the business, their specific needs, and the strategy you employed to address those.

ADVANTAGES OF BUSINESS STORYTELLING

Storytelling creates interest and curiosity. Stories add a level of humanity to what you do. They are a less corporate approach and turn decision-making into doing business with people, not a company per se. Stories get people's attention. Simply put, stories are more engaging than a list of facts, features, and benefits. That's one reason speakers use stories in their talks. They get and hold people's attention.

Storytelling is a powerful marketing strategy. People want to connect with businesses they can relate to, and stories, authentically told, are one of the best ways to create a connection.

Story is a filtering mechanism to attract the right clients. From a content marketing perspective, more people will consume story-based content. There's also an SEO benefit. You will get more traffic, engagement, and response.

HOW TO TELL AN AUTHENTIC STORY

Turn everything into a story. Think through your experience as a business owner, where everything is a story you can share. Anything can be an opportunity to put something out there. Make a note, add meat to the bones, and put it out into the world.

Be transparent. Don't be afraid to be honest about what you do or why and how you do it. That requires a certain comfort level with who you are and with your voice. You never want to be in a situation where you're just telling people what you think they want to hear.

That's why we created a section on our website about how much social media costs. We wanted to put things out that are helpful. That may not be best short term, but it will be long term as it filters out the price-shoppers. The fact is, this particular resource will most likely turn away as many prospects as it attracts, and that's okay. Don't let the fear of detracting people prevent you from putting out great stuff.

Telling transparent, authentic stories carries some dangers. For one, you will miss opportunities you might otherwise get. But, as I said, you can't be everything to everyone. Focus on producing great content that attracts the customers and clients you absolutely want, even if you risk pushing some away. Be yourself and work toward building a business you can feel good about. Leave no mystery about who you are.

There are also dangers when authenticity goes lacking. Tell an inauthentic story that does not truly represent you and your company, and you will fall prey to attracting clients or customers who aren't a good fit. It produces counterproductive relationships. You will become a "me-too" business instead of standing out from the crowd.

Put distribution channels in place. These can include a blog, podcast, video, social media, and more. Find the channel best suited to your personality and style. If you're good on camera, go with that. Perhaps writing is a better outlet for you. Regardless of the medium, the main point is capturing your stories and putting them out into the world.

The podcast I launched six months ago is a perfect example of storytelling. It's given me a platform to share insights about our business quickly and easily. I find a podcast is a great way to tell stories and create a repository of easily accessible content you can repurpose and reuse. (I talk much more about podcasting in Chapter Fifteen.)

Speaking of authenticity in storytelling, in one podcast episode, I talk about my divorce. It was a painful, expensive process. Later, I met a "collaborative" law group that uses mediation and negotiations to help couples settle out of court—but it was too late to take advantage of their process in my situation. Now, I'm super passionate about talking to attorneys who work collaboratively to prevent others from experiencing what I went through. It's my way of helping others not go down that path.

That personal story morphed into a business story. The guest for that episode was a collaborative family law attorney we have been working with for eight years. He talks about how much we transformed his business and how the power of my story and his came together to create great synergy.

EVERYTHING DOESN'T HAVE TO BE PERFECT

In my opinion, it's better if it isn't. Those rough edges make it feel real.

INCLUDE YOUR TEAM'S STORIES

As your business grows and you build a team, allow them to share their stories. Don't make the company just about you. Find opportunities for your team to participate and contribute.

HAVE A CALL TO ACTION

Every story you tell needs to have a "moral"—or, to put it in marketing terms, a call to action. This needs to tie back to something related to the products you sell or services you offer; it's not just about telling a story for story's sake. Tell the story and wrap it in lessons learned and a takeaway to inspire action.

Your story is the foundation of the business you will build and critical to developing trust and likability with your audience. The world is changing, and more and more people are consuming content and building relationships digitally than ever before. Make sure you get your stories right and out into the world.

PART 2

BUILDING AN
ANTI-AGENCY BUSINESS

CHAPTER FOUR

HOW TO BUILD AND SCALE A VIRTUAL BUSINESS

The Big Idea: Working in an office setting is a thing of the past. Virtual is the future. Here's how to set yourself up to run a successful remote-based business.

....

The pandemic has increased the velocity of the work-from-home (WFH) trend dramatically. While we were already on that path before the pandemic struck, the increased challenges of getting from place to place, the gained productivity from working remotely, and technology advances have collectively propelled virtual working to the forefront. One hundred years from now, people will think we were crazy to get in cars and sit in traffic for hours using precious natural resources, just to get to and from work!

Pre-Pandemic, only one in five (20 percent) of American employees worked from home. By December 2020, that number had shot up to over 70 percent, with 54 percent saying they wanted to continue once the pandemic ends. Many employees who were forced to return to an office environment have bounded together to push back against their company's leadership. Others have even opted to quit and pursue opportunities at companies that "get it."

Businesses were also forced to deal with preconceptions that being in a remote world would negatively affect productivity. Hundreds of studies debunk that notion and show productivity in a WFH environment rose measurably. One study, by Bloomberg, found that productivity in the US economy increased by 5 percent, primarily because of savings in commuting time. The Harvard Business Review said employees spend 12 percent less time being drawn into large meetings and 9 percent more time interacting with customers and external partners. A study by Stanford University of 16,000 workers over nine months found that working from home increases productivity by 13 percent.

Traditional businesses look at the negatives—fear of a drop in productivity, loss of camaraderie and socialization, and a lack of creativity that comes from face-to-face interaction. The truth is most companies simply don't like the perceived lack of control that comes with people being free to work from home. This is not a black-and-white issue. Still, people are getting used to the benefits of remote work, and the workforce demands that employers offer that flexibility.

Technology is aiding the remote work shift, making the transition much more seamless. Categories include everything from communication platforms (Slack and Microsoft Teams), to video meeting tech (Zoom and Cisco WebEx), to collaborative project management tools (Asana, Trello, and Basecamp), and more. Security has not been overlooked, either, thanks to multifactor authentication, use of VPNs, and call encryption.

That's why I would advise any business just starting to go virtual. There are too many benefits to a start-up company to think otherwise. You'll save a tremendous amount of time and money by doing so, and those are both resources you are going to need to build your business. There are exceptions, of course. Plenty of companies can't be fully remote or even remote at all—gyms, grocery stores, hair salons, and so forth. But the percentage of those that can will grow over time. Those that can but don't will fall behind.

SIZE MATTERS, BUT NOT THE WAY YOU THINK

When I started Socialistics, I chose to work from home. It was from a dollars-and-cents perspective at the time. I figured that, as the company grew, we would need to get an office. Being in the same room has many benefits, after all. That's what successful agencies do, I thought. It's the typical agency formula.

So, I got a physical address. I didn't want to lose an opportunity because of not having an office. I felt I needed to give the perception that the agency was bigger than it was. However, in doing so, I disguised who we really were. I wanted to be everything to everybody, not realizing that what I thought was a weakness was actually a strength. It comes back to authenticity. Your "weakness" can be your strength.

I found that, in fact, most clients prefer to work with a smaller agency, one where the owner is accessible. They feel like a boutique-size agency is more likely to be creative and not so black and white in what it does. I also found out that companies want to work with a young, hungry start-up that won't get complacent and will fight for the work. If a prospective client thought we weren't big enough, we decided it was not our client. We only wanted to go after those that looked at our size as an advantage. Once we embraced our true self, success followed.

Even though embracing your "smallness" is a good thing, you may not want to use your home address for privacy reasons, or simply because you don't want your business to show up in a residential environment. Kill two birds with one stone by finding a shared office space that offers one rate for having a professional address as well as access to the space to use as needed.

VIRTUAL OFFICE ENVIRONMENT BENEFITS

There are a huge number of benefits associated with working virtually:

LESS EXPENSIVE

Working virtually is much less expensive than running an office—a cost saving that can help you price more competitively and be more profitable. Plus, there's no travel expense for employees. They can live and work from anywhere in the world.

Many companies are doing that now, thanks to COVID, but we had a running start. At this point, I can't see why we would have a physical office. Not when we can leverage technology to stay connected and build rapport with employees and clients. It has not stopped us from winning business—90 percent of our prospects don't care.

INCREASED TALENT POOL

A virtual office environment means that the talent pools the employer draws from aren't limited to the immediate geographic area. Do you know how much easier it is to find great talent when you can cast your net globally? It's a game changer.

FREEDOM

During interviews, when candidates are asked what they value most in a new role, they often answer the same way: They want the freedom to work where and when they choose. To them, having that freedom is the most powerful thing in the world—even more important than money. These employees will often take less to have the freedom to live and work on their own terms rather than be restricted to specific hours or locations. Freedom is a business benefit that costs you nothing to offer but carries tremendous value.

BROADER BUSINESS HOURS COVERAGE

Because our employees are located across the globe, we have a unique situation where we can provide greater accessibility and responsiveness with people working at times of the day when others aren't. It provides a level of access we couldn't otherwise. I set expectations with the team about where and when it's needed and how to deliver it across the board.

ADDITIONAL DAY

For most people, working a traditional job comes with a multi-hour commute, usually on average two or more hours to work and back, and some even more. When I started my business, one of the most remarkable perks was the realization that, by not sitting in traffic, I literally had an extra day every week to work with. That in and of itself is worth it.

I cannot stress how powerful a virtual business is in today's market. It changes everything dramatically. It can lead to increased profit margins, the ability to hire top talent, and the running of a more successful business with employees who share your values.

You might ask, what about an established business that has an office? Why should it change?

While there are demonstrated models of success in running a virtual office, some companies are successful enough that they don't have to change from a physical office environment.

For those who wish to change, I advise creating a transitional period where employees work remotely two days a week—you can set up technology solutions to facilitate that—and make the transition slowly. Be prepared for hiccups along the way. Even with remote working growing at an astronomical rate, not everyone can handle it. So, make sure you have the right people in place: those with a self-starter mindset who don't need a lot of direction or hand holding to do their job.

It's likely that if you're already in a physical location, you either have a mindset of absolutely going remote or absolutely not. Either way, don't be on the fence. If your business success depends on it, you may have to do it to cut expenses to survive.

VIRTUAL OFFICE DISADVANTAGES AND CHALLENGES

Despite the many advantages, there are, admittedly, some disadvantages and challenges to working remotely.

SOCIALIZATION

You can miss out on the social aspects of an office environment, the camaraderie, those on-the-fly watercooler conversations that can lead to innovation and spark creative ideas. Working virtually will never replace that, so be prepared to come up with creative ways to leverage technology and prioritize digital opportunities to connect personally and professionally.

NOT WIRED FOR REMOTE

Not everyone is wired for remote work. Not everyone is self-sufficient or self-motivated, which makes a virtual office harder to manage. You need to hire for that by finding the people who are best suited to a WFH environment. I don't hire anyone unless I am confident they can handle this environment. People are growing up in a world where it's more of a norm. But it is more of a challenge for a workforce used to working in an office.

LOGISTICS

There are logistical issues with remote work. Time zone differences can be a challenge, for instance. You have to work around your employees' availability. However, I believe it's better to have the right people than worry about their location. You do have to ensure your people are accessible and responsive—that's the trade-off of living where you want and setting your own hours.

WORKFORCE SCALABILITY

Workforce growth is a challenge. Your org chart can't continue to be flat. Cultivate leadership who can manage a growing team. With our growth, the business became bigger than just me, and that required me to hire new employees and promote others to leadership roles. It depends on what you want your business to be—self-sustaining where you don't have to spend a lot of hands-on time (which probably means you won't grow beyond a certain level), or a "take over the world" kind.

TECH STACK

It takes time to figure out the right set of tools needed to run a virtual business with a remote workforce. It's a matter of trial and error. However, communication is vital, which, along with email, makes tools like Slack, Skype, or Microsoft Teams indispensable. Be willing to pay for the premium version of the software so you can take full advantage of what these tools offer.

TIME TRACKING

Tracking employee time can be a hassle, especially when they are scattered all over the globe. Still, it is necessary, especially in a service-based environment.

I hate to admit it, but I was anti-time tracking. Every agency I had worked for integrated it incredibly poorly. My dissatisfaction had more to do with lack of execution, however, than the need for it, but I didn't want to do it. It made my stomach turn just thinking about it!

Then, a year in, my company was growing and taking on additional staff. I realized we had to revisit the issue. (Actually, my leadership team decided that our business needed it.)

Integrating time tracking into our business has been eye-opening. It keeps people accountable and gives me excellent visibility as an informed business owner, not to check on people but to know how we're spending time. If we can find ways to utilize our time better, we become more efficient, not wasting time on a client giving away otherwise billable hours. The key to this working for us is picking the right technology and, more importantly, educating the team on the value it affords the business. When they believe in it, the accuracy and value grow tenfold, and they see it as an integral part of their job and our company's success.

HOW TO RUN A VIRTUAL OFFICE

- Hire well. It all starts with hiring people who are best suited to a WFH environment. If you don't have the right people, nothing else matters; if you are not equipped to do that independently, get help. Hire self-starters, people with an entrepreneurial spirit, and definitely those who value freedom above all other perks.

- Invest in tech. You need to set aside money in a budget that accommodates the necessary technology to empower your employees and business. Some of this will be trial and error. Test different tools and platforms to find what works best for you.

- Establish SOPs. Have standard operating procedures and processes for everything you do. You will figure it out as you go, but you can't just wing it. Create documentation so employees have something to work from. It helps with scale.

- Stay connected. It's easy to get lost in the work when you're not in the same place, so put opportunities to connect on the calendar. Have a rewards program in place like Bonus.ly. Focus on relationship building. Have some fun; camaraderie is necessary for success.

A virtual business can be very successful and highly profitable if you put the right pieces in place from the start. As your business grows and it becomes bigger than just you, you're going to need that infrastructure to ensure you can manage a remote team effectively, and it starts with having the right pieces in place.

CHAPTER FIVE

HIRE PEOPLE BETTER THAN YOU

The Big Idea: Finding, keeping, and cultivating the best talent can lead to business success.

....

"I was the third hire. My first invoice to Jason was $52, but I felt it was the start of something amazing." ~ Joanna, Director of Client Services

When you're first starting out, the business begins and ends with you. And it's likely that it's going to be that way for a while. But if you play your cards right, the time will come when the business becomes bigger than just you. That's where the magic really starts to happen. Making your first hire is exciting, but that excitement is accompanied by a lot of work. Finding great talent that you can trust and rely on is not easy. And those first few hires will be critical to the success of your business.

The biggest mental hurdle that you must overcome is the realization that you're going to have to eventually let go of many of the decisions and responsibilities you've grown accustomed to owning. To do that means surrounding yourself with people you can trust to do the work and inevitably run many aspects of the company.

Average or just okay employees will not cut it. They won't help you grow a business. Finding the right employees and mentoring and cultivating them is expensive and time consuming, but when you hire world-class talent, you don't have to do that as often. Not only will hiring average employees take more time and effort, but they also become a revolving door. It is highly profitable and timesaving to hire the right people. That's what a WFH remote virtual office setting we talked about earlier can enable you to do.

WHAT CONSTITUTES WORLD-CLASS EMPLOYEES?

When I think about what makes an employee world-class, it's not skill sets that come to mind but un-trainable traits like passion, energy, and drive. Those are the most valuable.

Untrainable traits are characteristics that people inherently have. They're born with them, or they were instilled in their lives at an early age in some way. It's who they are as people. It's how they live their lives. While these traits can certainly be refined or improved, typically they either exist or they don't. These are the areas I focus on when it comes to hiring world-class talent.

For example, are they great communicators? Are they passionate? Do they have an energy about them? An infectious personality? Are they a self-starter? Do they have an entrepreneurial spirit?

When assessing new talent, ask candidates what they deem most important. You're looking for them to tell you freedom, remote work, flexibility. If those top the list, there's a much greater likelihood they will stick around long term and stay loyal to you. Finding, training, and mentoring is time consuming and expensive, so the less you have to do it, the better!

You can teach someone to do a task, but you want a person who has those kinds of foundational elements over someone who has task-related skills but lacks the intangibles. That's a deal-breaker for me.

So, in reality, it's not world-class talent that I look for but world-class people. Those people will kick ass, fit into the culture, and have staying power. In a perfect world, they have both skills and the intangibles, but I opt for the intangibles over talent set every time.

ADVANTAGES WORLD-CLASS EMPLOYEES BRING TO A BUSINESS

If you hire people like those I have described, your business will be more profitable and run more smoothly. You won't be as tied to the day-to-day and will experience time savings as a result. They can take on added responsibilities as the business grows so that it runs more effectively and efficiently. Thanks to their proactive nature, they will identify gaps and opportunities for growth. You will see less attrition and turnover. You will be more attractive to clients and customers and more competitive in the marketplace.

For me, hiring world-class talent has translated to an improved quality of life and greater peace of mind. I know that my company is in capable hands and business is being taken care of. My team has become like my extended family.

CHALLENGES OF BUILDING A WORLD-CLASS TEAM

Surrounding yourself with people like these forces you to be a good leader. They challenge you. Give them extra support. It's an added responsibility.

However, the more significant challenge is finding these people. It takes time and persistence. Be picky. You can't just settle. Be willing to go the extra mile in pursuit of them.

You also have to pay them more, but they are worth it. So, bite the bullet and decrease profit margins if you need to, knowing that the high bar you set will pay dividends in the long run.

To be fair, the temptation to lower the bar always lurks around the corner. And I'm not saying every employee must meet such a high standard. It depends on the role.

For example, we have part-time folks who come in and prove themselves. There are areas where you can do that—tactical, operational, teachable areas—but, when it comes to other traits, I must see those I talked about earlier or we're wasting our time.

Folks like this also need a career path. They can't (and won't) stay in the same role forever. As the business owner, you need to make room for growth.

WORLD-CLASS TALENT TRAITS

Every business differs in what traits it considers a priority, but there are definitely some core ones that you should focus on regardless of what products or services you offer. Assuming your business is also going to be remote, these are the traits that we've found to be the most important.

COMMUNICATION

I don't care what business you're in, nothing is more worthwhile than a strong communicator. That skill transcends all roles. People who are good writers or who communicate well face-to-face are a tremendous asset. This skill should top your list of requirements for any new hire.

SELF-STARTER

You need to surround yourself with people who don't need any hand holding. Folks who after being on–boarded can take the ball and run with it. I absolutely love people who just get things done and are driven to do so with little to no direction. Time is as valuable as money, if not more, so surrounding yourself with self-starters is going to vastly improve your work–life balance and help your business thrive.

ALIGNED VALUES

More and more, people are putting a premium on associating with companies that align to their core values. Do you know yours? Are you putting them front and center on your website? Are you living them and can demonstrate them? Make sure you are, and, when assessing talent, don't settle for people who don't align with them. It won't end well.

GOOD PEOPLE

This may seem like a corny trait, but, ultimately, it may be one of the most important. The world is filled with all kinds of people, and when it really comes down to it, some are good, some not so good. Do they have a good heart? Do they genuinely care about other people and their well-being? Do they put others before themselves? Life is short, and your business is going to be one of the biggest parts of your life. Don't settle for assholes at any level. Surround yourself with good, caring, empathetic people, and your business will thrive because of it.

HOW TO FIND WORLD-CLASS TALENT

Have a fully vetted, well-written job description that gets at the heart of what the opportunity consists of.

Accompany that with a convincing page on your website that highlights the benefits of working for the company and what they are likely to experience. You're selling yourself to them as much as they are to you, so make your offering a strong pitch between what the role is and what the company offers. What makes your company unique? What is your culture? What are your core values? Tell your story, and you'll attract the right talent more efficiently.

The days of looking at résumés to find an appropriate candidate are over. Résumés don't carry as much weight as they used to. They're simply a check-the-box snapshot of their experience.

The best thing we ever did to make the hiring process more efficient was to create a system where we provide three to five very pointed questions that relate to what we're looking for regarding the role. We ask candidates to record a three-to-five-minute video answering those questions.

When someone records a video, you get a sense of their demeanor, energy, passion level, and communication ability. They do that, attach their résumé, and that's how they apply.

This approach enables us to weed out pretenders who apply to hundreds of jobs—they will not take the time to record a video—which saves us an enormous amount of time.

Weeding out 80 percent of applicants may seem like a bad thing, but it's not. You should only consider 20 percent of the applicants anyhow. That way, you don't end up with an endless stream of emails and phone conversations. If they have experience and emotional intelligence, chances are you know within five to ten minutes (maybe sooner) whether they have the potential to work at your company.

Out of that group, we identify those we feel are worthy of a Zoom interview. You need to see them in a face-to-face environment. The candidate doesn't show up on video? Red flag. It's a must in this new day and age.

Upfront, we ask questions that give us a sense of whether they can fit the role. We ask about their experience or examples of their work. The call is designed to get to know them as a person. Are they a good communicator? Are they well suited to our company culture? Are they proactive? Did they do their homework and appear interested? We look for signs of life that tell us this person wants the job and is a good fit for it.

One question we ask ourselves is, do I want to work with this person? If the answer is yes, then the answers to the other questions are yes. If you treat it that way, it's not that hard to determine.

I used to be on those calls, but now I turn that job over to people who understand our core values and have been with us long enough to know what I believe. They serve as an extension of me. I know they will treat those interviews with the same weight and approach as I would. Not to mention, they are the ones who will be working with them on a regular basis. Who better to truly assess fit than them?

When they have these conversations and say they want to bring the person on the team, I set up a call with the candidate. It's less of an interview and more of them getting to know me and me them. I don't want to be faceless but rather show that I am approachable. I am selling us on them as much as vice versa. By the time they get to me, it's usually already a yes, but, as the owner of the business, I feel it's important to still be part of the process and get to know those we bring on board.

Don't look for people exactly like you. Be open to and embrace diversity. I'm introverted, but I don't want to surround myself with a bunch of introverts! I need a few extroverts. I also need people who will challenge me. People with different experiences to round out the team and add depth and perspective.

"These are the questions we provide to potential hires" for example

1. WHEN IT COMES TO YOUR NEXT JOB OPPORTUNITY, WHAT ARE YOUR NONNEGOTIABLES?

2. WHAT IS YOUR SUPERPOWER? WHAT IS IT THAT YOU ARE BETTER AT THAN ANYONE ELSE THAT COMES INCREDIBLY NATURALLY TO YOU?

3. WHAT ARE YOU MOST PROUD OF IN YOUR LIFE, PERSONALLY OR PROFESSIONALLY?

4. TELL ME WHAT A FRIEND, A FAMILY MEMBER, AND A WORK COLLEAGUE WOULD SAY ARE YOUR GREATEST STRENGTH AND YOUR BIGGEST WEAKNESS.

5. IMAGINE SIX MONTHS FROM NOW YOU'RE FINISHING UP ON A FRIDAY AND THINK TO YOURSELF, TAKING THIS JOB WITH THIS COMPANY WAS ONE OF THE BEST DECISIONS I'VE EVER MADE. WHAT WOULD NEED TO HAVE HAPPENED DURING THOSE SIX MONTHS FOR YOU TO FEEL THAT WAY?

EMPLOYEES VS. CONTRACTORS

We've talked about the changing landscape of business and remote work, and that's affecting how businesses approach hiring. When you're just starting out, it can be much easier, lower risk, and affordable to bring folks in as contractors first. You limit the amount of time and effort spent on bringing people on, as well as limit your risk by being able to make sure people are a good fit. The fact is that more and more people want to be contractors rather than employees. It goes back to the pursuit of freedom. It allows them to be nimbler with their career, diversify their income streams, not be tied to any particular region, and treat their work as a business by writing off expenses. It's a win-win.

There are certainly benefits to hiring people as employees, however. While I still recommend starting with contractors, once people have proven their worth and are a good fit, transitioning them into a full-time role is a great way to send a message of commitment. It's also a way to have a bit more control over that person's exclusive commitment to your business versus juggling multiple opportunities. If your business is thriving, and you can afford the additional legwork and costs associated with full-time employees, go for it. Just be prepared for the complexities that come with it, including human resource tasks, taxes, benefits, and, if your business is national, the need to adhere to each state's specific laws where your employees live.

Check out Bonus.ly (www.bonus.ly). In addition to being an incredible morale-boosting rewards system for your virtual business, you can create tasks that your team can participate in to earn points that can then be exchanged for gift cards. It's a great way to incentivize your team to help with your recruiting!

PROMOTING A JOB TO ATTRACT WORLD-CLASS TALENT

When you promote a new job opportunity, go through the entire publishing process. Think about where the role is and the most likely place candidates exist. Also, reserve room in the budget for the process. Typically, we look in four places: LinkedIn, Glassdoor, Indeed, and Craigslist. Where we look depends on the role's complexity. Craigslist is high volume and less quality, so it's best for part-time or entry-level hires.

I don't recommend paying for individual LinkedIn job listings, especially if you are budget conscious or just starting out. If you have a company page, you can post for free, and everyone on the team can share it. You can also choose to throw a bit of money at promoting it, which is much cheaper than individual job post listings.

Use Indeed. It powers Glassdoor as well as several other web properties. That way, you get high volume at a relatively decent cost.

Our process vets that out. You will have to pay to post to get the volume of applicants needed to find the diamond among the coal.

Two other no-cost ways to consider: Tap into your professional network and post on social media. Spend a few bucks on Fiverr for someone to whip up some great-looking graphics that highlight your opportunities rather than the typical dull text or link posts. People are visual creatures, and so many job opportunities are promoted in a dull and nonvisual way.

Another way to find world-class employees is through referrals. I incentivize the team to bring people to us and to share company social media posts. They get a bonus for anyone we hire. Referrals are a vital lead source and often the best way. That doesn't negate the need to go through the interview process, but if a valued employee or client knows someone like them, that person could be a strong candidate.

My team and I also reach out personally to ask for referrals, as everyone posting helps.

Sometimes, we find the right person in a week; it can take a month at other times. You can't wait until you absolutely need someone, either, not for people of this caliber. Start two months out, even if that means bringing the person in sooner than you will need them. You can't plan for the right person; be comfortable bringing them on as soon as you find them.

Interns are another great way to bridge hiring gaps. If you have entry-level needs, I highly recommend giving college students or those early in their career an opportunity to test the waters with you. It's relatively risk free for both sides and potentially gives you a pipeline of future hires. However, don't expect "intern" to mean free anymore. Times have changed. Regardless of where your opinion lies on whether interns should be paid, it has become more common that they are. Quite frankly, I believe that to be a good thing.

WHAT WORLD-CLASS EMPLOYEES LOOK FOR IN A COMPANY

I find that people are motivated by five buckets: money, time, opportunity, leadership, and culture. These qualities round out what people want and what businesses need to nurture talent and keep them. I try to speak to each of those areas.

MONEY

Money isn't as important as it used to be, but we pay people what they are worth at a minimum. If you try and low-ball people, you're setting yourself up for a whole lot of employee/contractor attrition.

TIME

Time has become the most valuable commodity in the world. People are more mobile; they travel more. The younger generation is not tied to a home. They like having a job that gives them the freedom to spend time when and wherever they want. Creating an environment where you can provide that benefit costs you nothing, yet it offers great value to the right person. If handled appropriately, this can be the most valuable thing you provide your team, and it costs you nothing.

Need a great resource to open a pipeline of opportunities to hire or intern college students?

Check out Handshake (https://joinhandshake.com/)

"Jason lets us prioritize what's important to us. What's important to me is freedom. I moved from Texas to Australia, a decision made on a whim. To do that and know my job isn't going anywhere is the best thing in the world." ~ Joanna

OPPORTUNITY

World-class people need a path to growth and opportunity. If you provide it, they will stay with you for years to come. If you don't, they will find another path. Make it clear to those you bring on what is available to them and what the future can hold.

LEADERSHIP

World-class talent needs a world-class employer, a leader with whom they can identify and respect—someone they want to work for. A competent, compassionate, inspiring, high-energy, fair, equitable, knowledgeable, and experienced leader. Someone with a kind, considerate heart who is good to his or her people.

CULTURE

"It's definitely the people, the culture ... that is so addicting. The respect I get and give in return not only makes me a better employee, but a better person." ~ Joanna

It's vital to create an environment people want to be in—one that's fun, kind, generous, and inviting. You want people to want to be around others, even in a virtual setting, and that starts with culture.

You want to build a team aligned with those values. At first, our core values may not be the same for those I bring in, but they become their core values over time—they align to who they are as a person.

Ultimately, it's about happiness. Take pleasure in your work. Let it be a source of joy. If you can create that kind of culture, it's infectious and fosters an environment of loyalty.

Pay them what they are worth, give them the freedom to live and work where they want, surround them with people they love working with doing work they enjoy where they see a career path—those people ain't going anywhere!

I have all the confidence in the world that the folks on my team will more than likely stick around as long as I will have them. If I can create an environment like I have described above, I make it very difficult to leave!

It's not easy. It takes time. Be persistent. Growth will be slow, but it will be the right kind, one that provides stability.

"It's just been beautiful to create a company culture where people can thrive and grow. And while not everyone will be along for the ride long-term, I don't plan on going anywhere." ~ Ashley

CULTIVATING A WORLD-CLASS TEAM

Cultivating a team of world-class performers comes down to commitment. Give these new hires a thorough onboarding experience, map out your workflows, and have resources in place so they come in comfortably ramped up.

I have weekly one-on-ones with the leadership team. They work with extended teams, that don't report to me. However, I also meet with all the employees monthly. I am committed to having relationships with everyone on the team.

Have processes in place that make their path to promotion and earning increases clearly defined. Not everyone cares about that—they are happy doing the job they were hired for. Understanding their wants—what's important to them—that's what the one-on-ones are for. I'm a real person to them, not some high-level CEO who leads with an iron fist. I'm approachable.

It shows you care about them, that they are a priority, and that their well-being is important to you. You create an environment that supports them. You provide opportunities for continued education where they can improve in knowledge and skill. An environment that allows them to pursue knowledge and excellence keeps us ahead of the curve.

We also celebrate individual achievement where employees can reward each other for doing great work. It inspires them to continually improve. It contributes to a culture of accountability, generosity, recognition, and reward.

Seeing my team's appreciation for what they have is the inspiration for this book. It's what I believe every business leader should emulate.

CHAPTER SIX

BUILDING YOUR BACK OFFICE EFFICIENTLY AND AFFORDABLY

The Big Idea: A back office enables your business to scale so you can focus on those activities you are best suited to.

....

As your business grows, you will need to put foundational items and resources in place—tools, tech, and services—that allow things to run more efficiently and affordably, enabling you to focus on what you are best at—strategic activities that drive business growth—and relieve you from dealing with tasks where you lack expertise. That means building a back office.

That's where many entrepreneurs make a mistake. They get caught up in the fear of spending money, so they do everything themselves when they could devote a small amount, comparatively speaking, to outsourcing work through affordably priced support or use of technology platforms.

Don't get me wrong, you need to hustle and grind out of the gate, and in most cases, do everything—not only from a resource standpoint but also to gain experience so that when you start to outsource, you can ensure others get it right.

I was doing my own bookkeeping for a while, using an accounting resource for self-employed people. I was decent at it, but in trying to carry out all the financial aspects of the business on my own, I made mistakes.

So, I inquired about what it would cost me to let the accounting firm take over the bookkeeping: a whopping seventy-five dollars per month! I signed up immediately. Why should I be spending time doing that when I needed to focus on strategic business growth? What would take me an hour takes them fifteen minutes. Find experts in these areas and let them do the work, whether that's accounting, legal, HR, or whatever the need may be. Get some of that experience initially but get comfortable parsing out the tasks you aren't best at or passionate about.

Looking for an accounting/ bookkeeping resource when you're just getting started? Check out The Collective (www.collective.com), an excellent, affordable option for solopreneurs or small companies.

Here's another example.

I record a podcast every two weeks. When I started, I did everything—recording, editing, publishing, promotion—the whole bit. After a while, the initial excitement wore off, and it got harder and harder to keep up with. However, I knew I needed to keep doing it, so I found someone affordable who could take over the technical aspects that I didn't have the time or inclination for. Now, I can't just outsource the whole thing. It needs to be me on these podcasts managing conversations and interviews, but all that editing and technical stuff? No thanks. The person I hired can do a much better job than me and more efficiently, too. Now, doing the podcast is much more scalable. I just show up and hit record. I'm spending some money each month, but it works because it's one less thing I have to think about and makes the chances of sticking with it that much more likely. As Benjamin Franklin famously said, "Time is money."

Now, my mentality has changed from doing everything myself to save money (which actually costs me more) to deciding what I can get off my plate that will enable me to open my mental capacity to things that I'm best suited to.

TWO TYPES OF INVENTORIES

There are two types of inventories when it comes to time: the amount you spend collectively—forty, fifty, sixty hours a week—and the other way, measuring productivity. In an agency, it's not just about the number of hours, but the number of things you're responsible for managing.

On average, I probably put in fifty to sixty hours per week, easy. The fatigue I feel isn't the hours but the volume of things I am required to pay attention to—thirty or forty different activities and projects that I'm popping in and out of over the course of a day. I'm constantly shifting gears. The same is true for many of my staff, especially the leadership team. My people have many things to attend to, like me, so I can't measure productivity based on only the number of hours; I also need to account for the number of tasks they are responsible for managing.

If someone is full time and putting in thirty-five hours per week, it is not an alarm bell for me. There is a big difference between doing the same thing for fifty hours and doing twenty things for thirty hours. Jumping in and out of things, juggling things, can be stamina draining. At a minimum, it's an equal amount of output.

Let me illustrate my point.

Part of the appeal of running your own business is that, in theory, you have the freedom to do whatever you want when you want. I had always wanted to learn to play the piano, and I figured, hey, I can find a half hour every day in my schedule to take this on, right? So, I bought a piano and started taking virtual lessons. Certainly, I could stick to a half hour a day long term to learn how to play. And while I had no problem finding the time, I couldn't turn my business brain off, which affected my ability to learn. It became a drag and a source of stress and anxiety. The amount of shifting gears with all that I was juggling in the business didn't allow me to truly "unplug" and focus on the piano. Even though I had time, I lacked the mental capacity to take on another thing.

That's when I realized ...

Your capacity isn't only determined by the amount of time you spend on things, but the number of things you spend time on.

I decided then and there that it's better to be great at less than average at everything. That's also when I decided to create a back office that would allow me to make the best use of my time.

BACK OFFICE FAQS

Let's break down what we mean by a back office and why having one in place is essential.

What is a back office, and why do you need it?

A back office simply consists of the tools, technology, and services that allow you to scale your business to run more efficiently and affordably, enabling you to focus on things you are best at and where your attention is needed most. Usually, that's the strategic and sales side of the business.

Having a back office keeps you from being drawn into too many overwhelming areas or where you lack the experience and necessary skills—the operational, tactical stuff that bogs you down with tasks you don't understand or can't do efficiently.

How important is it to not worry about things getting done?

As a new business owner, more than likely you will have to do everything at first. But there will come a time as the business grows when you hit a wall. When you reach that point, you should only do those things you are best at. You can't spend time on tactical activities you can easily outsource. Think more strategically and spend time where you bring the most value, where you can work on your business, not in it.

Make a list of all the tasks you're doing for the business, then go through and check all those that are outsourceable, whether shifted to another employee, a contractor, or a service provider.

What kind of things can you outsource?

The range of tasks you can outsource runs the gamut from bookkeeping, accounting, taxes, and legal to content creation (i.e., blog posts, e-books, videos, etc.) to marketing. The list is endless. Regarding content, there's a good chance that as business momentum builds, you will not have time to create as much as you should. Find trusted resources that can create content that represents you well.

CHALLENGES TO BUILDING A BACK OFFICE

Get comfortable with lower profit margins to put a back office in place. There are typical hard costs, so, as your business grows, the cost percentage ratio diminishes.

There will also be trial and error. Test and find the right mix of technology and resources that work for your business. You won't get it right every time. Use software demos and trials. Patience and stamina are called for, along with the right mindset.

Building a back office involves both technology and service. The above applies to tech and service-based businesses, be it accounting, legal, or HR. Find those who work well with you and vet them out.

Also, be prepared to become the subject matter expert when it comes to these areas. Take time to get up to speed and develop a process for how to incorporate the use of these tools and resources. Become well informed and comfortable, figure out how they connect to your business, and translate them into SOPs so that when new people come on, they have help in navigating the resources you have in place.

OUTSOURCING SERVICE PROVIDERS VS. HIRING IN-HOUSE

Starting out, you may have no other choice than to use outsourced providers. Hiring employees is time consuming and more expensive. With employees, you run the full gamut of expenses: taxes, benefits, vacation time, and so forth. As a new business owner, it makes more sense to lower your risk and take on resources that have more flexibility. Not to mention, we live in a whole new world. There are plenty of talented folks who are happy working on a contingency basis, either as a freelance service provider (think copywriter, graphic designer, programmer, virtual assistant) or contractor.

If the need doesn't warrant that much volume, outsourcing makes sense. It's less expensive and easier to implement than hiring employees. There are disadvantages, of course. Outsourced providers may not be as accessible as employees, and they are free to juggle multiple opportunities. Also, be careful in how you manage contractors. Treat them too much like a traditional employee and you can set yourself up for potential risk of penalties or fees from local government.

Regardless, outsourcing definitely has its advantages. It's less expensive, for one. At the very least it allows you to pay more for the help you need while not bearing the expense of traditional employees. There is less upfront risk. You can test folks out to make sure they are a good fit before committing too much time and resources.

WHEN TO SET UP A BACK OFFICE

You will know you need to set up a back office when there is not enough time in your day to get everything done. When you have grown in profitability—reached a certain threshold in revenue—so that you can afford to hire outsourced providers, identify what you can outsource or offload to someone else. Otherwise, your business will suffer by your inability to do it well.

STEPS TO SETTING UP A BACK OFFICE

Determine your needs. Know what you need to be prepared to do and where and when to get help when the business becomes bigger than you.

Find the right resources. Find the technologies and services that best serve your needs through vetting and testing. Get demos for technology platforms. Run through trials. Use them in the real world to make sure they're the right fit. Make sure they work for your business.

Map out processes and SOPs. Map out a process of how you will use these resources and establish SOPs for new hires as part of onboarding.

Focus on what you do best. With the resources in place, you can focus on your strengths—growing the business, sales, and marketing.

BACK OFFICE OUTCOMES

You will experience greater efficiency, peace of mind, and clearer focus. It empowers your team when they know they're supported. The result is greater productivity for you and your team.

There's an added benefit I should mention. At Socialistics, we have become a trusted advisor to clients. Often, they are going through the same challenges as we did. We recommend what works for us, provide guidance around business development, and serve as a resource. The better we get at running our business, the more our clients trust and rely on us.

Remember what I said earlier: Your capacity isn't only determined by the amount of time you spend on things but the number of things you must spend time on.

Build a back office and get more done.

For a complete and updated list of tools and resources we have used and continue to use to help us grow and manage our business, visit **www.socialistics.com/anti-agency-tools.**

You need to have the right tools and services to help support your business, and the reality is, you're going to experience trial and error with many of them. Don't worry about being perfect, and give different services and solutions a trial run to see what fits and works best for your business. And when all else fails, lean into those you know who've been there, done that who can give you experienced insights to make the right choices.

CHAPTER SEVEN

HOW TO BUILD YOUR SUPPORT STRUCTURE

The Big Idea: You need mentors, colleagues, and partners to scale a successful business. Here's how to find them, treat them, and keep them.

....

The most effective leaders are those who recognize they don't know everything. You must always be learning and creating opportunities to make that happen. It's easy to become tunnel-visioned with what you do, but to be effective, you need allies to converse with, learn from, and get coached by—people who can help you get out of your own way.

SUPPORT SYSTEM MAKEUP

An effective support system consists of a mix of mentors, colleagues, partners, groups (e.g., mastermind groups, LinkedIn groups), and like-minded organizations.

MENTORS

A mentor is someone accessible to you for questions or one-off conversations. They have been there, done that, and are further along the path than you. They provide the insight you wouldn't have otherwise. In most cases, a mentor is someone with whom you've built a relationship throughout your personal or professional life. Someone who is familiar with you and your background.

COLLEAGUES

It's helpful to surround yourself with people who are going through the same things as you. They are valuable to engage with and to share your stories and what you're doing with. Undoubtedly, you will find common threads. They may be on the tail end of an experience you are just entering into and can provide advice and support—or the other way around. It's a reciprocal relationship.

PARTNERS

No matter what your business is, a high probability exists that there are complementary services to it. We often get asked about things outside of our primary service areas. If you've surrounded yourself with partners, you can learn and exchange information so that instead of saying no, you can speak to a client's concerns as a subject matter expert and increase your value. When done right, this can be a consistent source of new business for you.

GROUPS

A group puts you in a collaborative environment with like-minded individuals. Searching those out and becoming a member is an excellent start to developing relationships. Groups can come in many different forms, including in-person networking groups, digital groups like LinkedIn or Meetup, or mastermind groups specific to your industry.

SUPPORT SYSTEM ADVANTAGES

A psychological component comes with running your own business. You can feel as if you're on an island, apart from conversations with team members in a digital environment using tools like Slack.

As a business owner, I'm going through things the rest of my team isn't. I have to concentrate on meeting payroll, providing benefits, concerning myself with what the business will look like in six months—things that create pressure and anxiety for me alone.

I can't let issues like these flow downstream to my team, only upstream to my support network. That's why I need help from individuals who have experienced the same things I'm going through. If you talk about them with your team, it could create unnecessary worry and anxiety. It puts them in an uncomfortable position. I won't do that, and I don't have to, thanks to the network I have built. While I'm certainly very transparent with my team, you must tread carefully to not be overly transparent; you need a support system that you can speak openly and freely with.

Good business owners get in front of problems. A support system gives you that resource. You feel better knowing you have people you can relate to who are in the same boat as you. I have learned tactics, strategies, tools, and resources I may not have been acquainted with otherwise or that it would have taken much longer to figure out on my own.

Not finding a group that meets your needs? Start one on LinkedIn or Facebook. It costs you nothing other than your time. If you have the patience and persistence, starting a group can be a great thought leadership move, and actually help position you and your business as an authority to others. It can also lead to new business opportunities with potential partners.

HOW TO FIND BUSINESS SUPPORT GROUPS

There are several ways to find groups. LinkedIn has many. There's also Meetup and Facebook. Do a Google keyword search for who you are and what you do, and you should find several that fit the bill. Retargeting ads will start to show up, too, pointing you in their direction. You'll also come across these organically as your business grows. It becomes a combination of looking for them and them finding you.

Once you find a group to join, make the time commitment to cultivate and maintain the relationships you form there. One key is to give and take in equal amounts.

I knew that I wanted to find a support system, but I wanted to be sure I had something to give, not just take. You set yourself up for success when you have that attitude. No one wants to be associated with folks who are only in it for themselves.

JOIN A MASTERMIND GROUP

I cannot stress highly enough the benefits you will receive from joining a mastermind group. Find those that pertain to what you do. They exist, although they are often niche- or industry-focused. In my case, I found a group exclusively for digital marketing agency owners called Digital Agency Elite. I had conversations early on in my agency life, but it wasn't until I felt I had something to give that I pulled the trigger. But I knew from day one, this was the group that made sense for me, and it's been one of the best decisions we've made as a business.

Are you an agency owner? I highly recommend the Digital Agency Elite Mastermind Group (https:// jasonswenk.com/ mastermind-invited/) run by Jason Swenk. It has been by far one of the best investments we have made as a business, and I couldn't have made it to where I am today without it.

WHAT IS A MASTERMIND GROUP?

Mastermind groups are the Holy Grail of business support systems. Conceptually, they are filled with experienced, intelligent business professionals. Members join for support, accountability, and to sharpen business leadership skills. There are also social interaction and business development opportunities. You must be committed to active participation, and there's often a fee to join. This is a good thing because it weeds out those just looking for free advice. If other like-minded business owners are paying to participate, then it's very likely it's a worthwhile investment. It's not a networking or coaching group, not a class. Everyone is on an equal footing regardless of business size or income.

These sorts of groups usually consist of a variety of different types of business owners—some new, some old, some small, some large. Everyone's situation is a little different.

Most groups have a similar type of format to the one we are in. We have two calls per week. We also use Slack and have subgroups within the larger body. The groups offer opportunities to get together in person to ask questions and build connections at a deeper level. There are referral opportunities, too. Everyone is there to help each other out. We're almost like a team looking out for each other's best interests. Often, these groups will have in-person get-togethers on a regular basis, as well.

Since joining, I have learned about integrated processes and tech solutions the group has recommended that have helped our business grow and become more efficient more quickly. I've also learned strategies: things others are doing that have proven successful. And I have gained peace of mind. It's comforting to know there is a group to fall back on when I have questions or needs.

I get excited about sharing what we've done with our agency that's worked. It's like gift-giving. You get more enthused about giving than getting, but it's a reciprocal relationship that benefits every member.

MY ADVICE ON JOINING A MASTERMIND GROUP

Joining a mastermind group is all about timing. As I said, there are usually costs associated with joining. For quality ones, it's not cheap, but it's worth every penny if you put as much into it as you take from it. You need to reach a point where you cross the threshold into a successful business and know it will not fail. Once you get over that hump and feel you have sufficient experience to bring value, then you're ready. Until then, you're not. Wait until you can offer something of worth. For those just starting out, I'd recommend finding free Facebook or LinkedIn groups that consist of folks in your industry.

SEEK OUT A MENTOR

A common thread in my life from the time I was a kid was my need to be a leader. My mom, a single parent, raised me, and I helped raise my younger brother. As a result, I grew up more quickly than most. I have always taken care of myself throughout my life, which forged in me the desire to be in control of my situation. It was a foundational stepping stone to who I am today.

In school, there weren't many teachers who influenced my life in a significant way. For most of my time, I never felt I was getting the mentoring, guidance, or leadership I needed. I was on my own. That had a lot to do with me always wanting to do my own thing and feeling my reach exceeded my grasp. I never felt life allowed me to take that risk.

Unfortunately for me, I didn't have many folks throughout my life who provided any meaningful mentorship opportunities. But that doesn't mean you shouldn't pursue them; quite the opposite. I wish I had taken mentors more seriously and pursued them because my ascent into entrepreneurship would probably have gone a little smoother. And maybe faster.

However, I did get to experience a great mentor later in my career. I had finally come across a manager who provided real value to me. He believed in me. I felt comfortable taking risks knowing he had my back. Working for him was the first time I ever felt safe—like he cared about me and cared for my well-being. He valued what I brought to the table. I wasn't going to be let go for some stupid reason. The stability I had been looking for, I found there. At least temporarily.

It shows that great leaders care about their people, and being compassionate is such a powerful mindset. To me, it is the most important thing in business and the key to success. A lot of that came from him.

BECOMING A MENTOR

As you grow as a business owner, you can inherently provide value to others. Being a mentor helps you create a sphere of influence that can lead to business growth.

What makes a good mentor?

A mentor has lots of business experience and something to offer. A mentor cares about their mentee's welfare and is passionate about helping.

If you want to mentor others, set ground rules on what that looks like for you time-wise. Can you handle one person? Two? More than two? It comes down to how much time you are willing to dedicate to act in that capacity. Sign up for opportunities that show the availability of time that you're comfortable with. Speaking opportunities are a benefit, as are testimonials. Lots of good can come from these.

If you take the approach and mindset of being helpful to others, I promise you good things will find their way to you. It can also open doors to partnerships in a variety of ways. Surround yourself with people who can help you. I'm an introvert and a loner. I was built for the pandemic! But after six months, even I needed some human interaction, so I pulled the trigger and invested in a mastermind group of agency owners.

Get comfortable with that investment and have a service mindset. If you help others with no expectation of anything in return, good things will come your way.

Be confident but not arrogant. You don't know everything, so be open-minded and willing to learn. Despite twenty-four years of experience, I still seek to learn from others.

Learn as much as you can, provide help as often as you can, and you will build a support system that is second to none!

CHAPTER EIGHT

WHY LEARNING TO SAY NO WILL TRANSFORM YOUR BUSINESS

The Big Idea: Don't take on every prospective client or customer who comes your way, and get rid of those who aren't suitable. It doesn't pay to waste time and resources on bad fits.

....

About six months into launching our agency, I took a flyer on a prospective client—I'll call him "Jim"—who I wasn't entirely sure would be a good fit. Still, I figured we'd give it a shot. We were a new business and needed everything we could get, a typical scenario for any business just getting started.

Jim was in the legal industry and was a little rough around the edges when it came to communication skills, but I knew how to navigate that.

I had no doubt that if Jim trusted the process, we could deliver results. However, it didn't take long before several red flags started flying. Jim didn't trust the process, routinely interfered with work, slowed down progress, and allowed unrealistic expectations to cloud his judgment. I or my team can often work though that, but the nail in the coffin was the repeated disrespect he regularly demonstrated to my team. It became clear at that point that he had to go. While our company was still relatively young and needed the revenue, I have a zero-tolerance policy for assholes. Nobody treats my team poorly and disrespectfully. Needless to say, we cut ties.

You may have to take every client or customer you can when you're starting out. The goal is to get to where you are empowered to say no, taking only those who are the best fit. Those who aren't can cause more damage than they are worth. Whether it's clients treating your team poorly, demanding more than what they are paying for, being unresponsive or unrealistic, whatever the reason, you cannot abide that behavior and expect to succeed.

In the beginning, you are trying to be everything to everybody and as a result will take on more risky clients or customers. That's okay. It's part of the process but can quickly become unmanageable. The great thing, though, is that each of those experiences will help you get better at vetting future opportunities more successfully. When you're just starting out, your instincts on good-fit clients and customers aren't as mature as they will become over time. As those experiences pile up, you'll eventually get to a point where you'll know pretty quickly when someone isn't a good fit. Trust the process. Be true to yourself and figure out when a situation is a no. It's not always black and white. Uncertainty can exist. Over time, you will learn to abide by your instincts.

WHAT THE POWER OF NO INVOLVES

The Power of No involves several elements. The first: having your team's back. That's especially necessary when you work in a virtual office environment.

You expect team members not to overreact when a client is out of order, but you need to protect them. The longer you allow a situation to fester, the worse it will get. Your job as the leader is to be your team's defender. You must draw a line between dealing with difficult client/customer situations (which is normal) and recognizing when those situations become unsustainable.

The added benefit of getting this right is increased team morale. When your team sees you have their back and are willing to put them first, you foster loyalty in your workforce. Replacing rock-star employee(s) is much more difficult than finding new clients.

> *"When I worked with other agencies, when you lost a client, all hell broke loose. Here, it's not what did you do wrong, it's about supporting you. He will fire a client if they mistreat us. Normally, if a client is paying, they stay with us no matter what. Here, it's people before profits." ~ Joanna*

You also have to learn to stand up for yourself and push back. In those cases, the client will either back down or double down. If they back down, perhaps you can course-correct and move forward. However, experience has taught us that, unfortunately, the relationship will not work most of the time. "Bully" clients are no different than bullies in everyday life. They will aggressively push their will and agenda on you to get their way. That is, until you push back.

The Power of No involves the freedom to say no from the outset before engaging with a client if something doesn't feel right. That's where true strength, confidence, and courage come into play—combatting an opportunity that may be moving toward a transaction, but your instincts tell you this is not going to work. The narrative is how to get out in front of problems before they happen. Saying no after is easier, but it's better to do it from the get-go.

We use the Power of No in our marketing to filter out those clients who aren't a good fit. We ask: "Are you ready for Socialistics?" and include bullet points. We ask pointed questions that, in truth, are designed to have a potential client say no. It's an incredibly powerful tool to help pick the right clients. There's also an added benefit: People often want what they perceive they can't have. When you approach it from that perspective, it creates desirability. It builds on Robert Cialdini's principle of scarcity; not everyone can work with us.

CHARACTERISTICS OF A BAD CLIENT

Typically, it boils down to two scenarios: Either the client is not ready for what you have to offer, or they are difficult to work with. In either case, explain sincerely and honestly why it's not a good fit and move on. That's hard to do, but it's necessary to get to that place to grow a successful business. Otherwise—and believe me when I tell you—the collateral damage will exceed whatever they spend with you.

There's another unintended benefit to telling clients no up-front. In many cases, they'll want to work with you even more. Chalk this one up to reverse psychology ... everyone wants what they perceive they can't have. While you may still want to stick to your guns, sometimes saying no can turn a lukewarm opportunity into a hot one.

THE "NOT READY FOR YOU" CLIENT

By "not ready," I mean that the client doesn't have the components in place for your offering to deliver the results you would expect.

We are a social media agency. If their website is horrible or their products and services aren't unique, good marketing can't fix that. If they aren't comfortable with the budget, that's not going to work. If they are impatient—it takes time for the things we do to bear fruit—that won't work. And if you engage with them and things don't work because of reasons like these, you're still going to get blamed for those failures.

Ultimately, when you are honest with a potential prospect about what they really need, and it's not you just yet, they will respect you more and will most likely return when they are ready.

THE DIFFICULT CLIENT

There are some crappy people in this world, and you don't want to be doing business with them. They may be disrespectful and treat your team poorly. It can become toxic, exposing your team to unnecessary problems.

Much like my earlier story of a client we had to fire, we had another individual who, on the surface, seemed like a good person. Once we got into a working relationship, however, we began to see signs of disrespect for some team members. The person did not view them as equals, was verbally abusive, and treated them like garbage. That's something for which I have zero tolerance.

As soon as I caught wind of what was happening, I got on the phone with the client and said I appreciated the opportunity to work with him, but I didn't feel like it was a good fit, that I have no patience for my team being treated poorly, and that we would be severing ties with him. He was stunned to have someone call him out and put him in his place. This goes back to what I mentioned earlier … showing strength and pushing back will stop bullies dead in their tracks. Sometimes you have to fight fire with fire. Doing so will feel empowering, and your business will benefit because of it.

Always set up your contracts with terms that allow you to end relationships for any reason. His revenue was not worth my team being treated poorly. You will find yourself in similar situations where that is the case for you, too.

"We had a client who was unhappy with the service that he was getting. Whether that was due to us or his expectations, it was kind of irrelevant. Ashley and I and another team member got on a call with him, and he was just incredibly disrespectful, was very unprofessional, and spoke to us really poorly. We got on a call with Jason after and told him, 'We've never felt so disrespected before in a work environment.'

"There were no questions asked. Jason said, 'My staff has been disrespected. That's the end of the line for this client. We're not going to work with them.' I think that was one of the most memorable and impression-making moments for me working at Socialistics. And that, to me, solidified the fact that this is not a normal agency. It doesn't even feel like it's an agency. It is the healthiest thing I've ever experienced, and it makes me want to work harder." ~ Joanna

Sometimes you need to enact the Power of No before they even become a client.

We had a sales call with a prospective client where we did a pitch. Up to that point, I was dealing with a particular person throughout the process and had several very productive conversations. A promising opportunity indeed. Come pitch day, my contact pulled in the company's marketing director, who had not been involved in the process.

We went through the pitch, giving them precisely what they had asked for. In the end, I paused and asked the marketing director what she thought. To put it mildly, she ripped us a new one.

"I don't see how this proposal has anything to do with us," she barked. "Where's the strategy? Where is the analysis of our current efforts?" She continued to be petty, insulting, and disrespectful in her delivery of feedback.

I calmly explained that this was a proposal for the services we offer with some general insights, and that we charge for strategy as most agencies would. I also followed that up with the fact that we were delivering exactly what had been discussed. Our contact meekly chimed in, agreeing, but I could sense this was not going to go anywhere.

I should have exercised the Power of No right then and there because I knew it would not work out, but I didn't. I sucked it up, pressed on through the rest of the pitch, and recovered a bit, agreeing to follow up in a few days. After discussing with the team afterward, even if we, miraculously, had won the business, we didn't have any interest in working with someone like that. So, I made the decision to simply email my contact, thanking them for the opportunity but saying we felt it was in everyone's best interests if they looked elsewhere for their needs. I'm pretty sure she read between the lines. And quite frankly, it felt good to say no.

Could we have done things differently with the prospect to cause a more positive reaction? Possibly. I could have found out who would be on the call and their role in the decision-making process. Also, we could have included the marketing director in any correspondence before making the pitch. It's possible she felt disenfranchised and left out, which may have led to her reaction.

Would I have loved that revenue? Sure. Could we have done a good job? Absolutely. Would we want to work with her? No way. That's the Power of No.

DISADVANTAGES OF KEEPING A BAD CLIENT

I have already alluded to a couple of disadvantages. Here is a more extensive list.

TEAM MORALE

A less than ideal client can kill your team's morale, leading to dissatis-faction, poor productivity, absenteeism, and even turnover. When employee engagement levels drop, so do profits.

IMPACT ON YOUR REPUTATION

If it's a situation where the client gets in their own way, and we're not able to produce results, it will lead to a split eventually and leave a bad taste in the client's mouth. It will harm your reputation whether it's your fault or not.

WASTED TIME

Bad clients can be a time-suck, pulling you into things outside your scope and preventing you from spending time working with your ideal clients.

WITHHELD REVENUE

There is some risk of clients withholding payment when they get into a bad situation. We get in front of that and end the relationship on our terms before it has a chance to go south.

HOW TO TELL GOOD FROM BAD

Telling a good prospective client from a bad one isn't always easy, nor is it always objective, but subjective instead—a gut feeling you get about the person's demeanor that tells you something isn't right and it won't work out.

You can add a tangible, analytical component, however. In our case, we ask a series of questions, which we couple with a pitch score from one to ten, with ten being perfect and one being no way.

Some situations are definitely a no and others an absolute yes. It's those in the middle where uncertainty lies. That's where real courage comes in. If it's a fifty/fifty proposition, I say walk away. Go after the ones that have a higher propensity to be a good fit. We need at least an eight to pursue the prospect further. It gives us a system of checks and balances that combines both the subjective/intuitive and analytical sides.

Even from day one, you have to exercise the Power of No. Don't take clients you know won't work. If starting out, take a chance on the fifty/fifties. Just make sure you can comfortably walk away.

HOW TO KNOW WHEN TO FIRE A CLIENT

How do you know when it's time to fire a client? Look for a pattern of behavior and trust your team to let you know when they have done all they can to satisfy the client's needs within the project scope.

Here's our approach:

- Have a sincere discussion with the client, giving them an opportunity to course correct.
- Take whatever steps you think are necessary to make things work.
- If you can't make it work, explain your reasons.

If you have a legally binding contract, you should have exit language so there will be no legal ramifications. The time window depends on the severity of the issue; thirty days is typical, but if the situation demands it, end the relationship quickly. Get in front of the problem before it has a chance to erupt.

CLIENT SELECTION ACTION STEPS

In addition to what I have already advised, here are some action steps to ensure you retain only the best-fit clients:

ASSESS THEIR DIGITAL FOOTPRINT

What does their website look like? Is the product or service interesting? Do they have a story to tell?

FILTER INBOUND REQUESTS

Carefully filter inbound requests from prospects. When you do this long enough, you will avoid wasting time putting in the work to make a pitch.

DON'T GO AGAINST YOUR INTUITION

Nine times out of ten, my intuition is correct. While it's possible I would walk away from a situation that could have worked out, for every one of those, there will be nine that didn't. It's not worth getting that one to have to deal with the other nine. Trust your instincts.

BRING YOUR LEADERSHIP TEAM INTO THE CONVERSATIONS

They are the ones doing the work, after all. Bring them into introductory calls and sales pitches. Involving your leaders is an added benefit for you and them. You get reinforcement, and they get ownership. So, involve them as much as you can.

ENFORCE A ZERO-TOLERANCE POLICY

Taking a long time to break off a relationship with a troublesome client will do your team and your business more harm than good. Show your team that you respect them and that you expect clients to respect them by having a zero-tolerance policy.

The Hartford Insurance company offers some excellent insights on how to fire a bad client that also includes several scripts. It may be worth your time to check out. (https://sba.thehartford.com/business-management/business-questions/fire-horrible-client/)

PERMIT YOURSELF TO JUST SAY "NO"

When you're starting out, it's tempting to take on everyone. I understand that from a revenue standpoint when you are building a client base. But, as soon as possible, give yourself the freedom and permission to exercise the Power of No. It's the best option for the long run.

Saying no to new business is not easy. Especially in the beginning. And what you can and can't say no to will evolve as your business grows. But trust me when I say it's incredibly empowering to get to a place where you can confidently say "no" to business. Choosing the right clients and customers is the real way to grow your business in a way that can scale, and it ensures that your team is set up for happiness and success.

> *"We want to bring on clients not just for the money but who will work well with us and give us creative freedom; with clients who are disrupting their industry and being the 'anti' in their world, not just pushing their product out. There's meaning behind the work they are doing; it's not just about making money, but about impacting the lives of the audience." ~ Ashley*

CHAPTER NINE

EMPOWERING YOUR TEAM SO YOU CAN WORK ON THE BUSINESS, NOT IN IT

The Big Idea: Thinking your ideas are the best and marrying yourself to them is a recipe for disaster. Be open to your team's ideas and willing to pivot if the results aren't there.

....

One of the most practical steps I've taken to grow my business, which is now part of my philosophy, is to hire people smarter than me and get out of their way.

If you surround yourself with people smarter than you, trust them, and let them pitch ideas about business growth—even if they fails—you will be better off.

My team helps me navigate my approach to leadership, business operations, and sales and marketing. They have an ownership stake, and their voice matters. Many agency and business owners don't think this way but are very authoritarian. I want my team to feel like we're doing this together, succeed or fail.

I consistently involve them and get their feedback regarding what's working and what's not. I'm also extremely transparent with my feelings. I don't just put on a happy face all the time. If I have a bad day, I share that. I want to be a real person to them. Who I am in my personal life is who I am as a business leader. There is no incongruity. I acknowledge my weaknesses and shortcomings—I'm not right all the time. My team knows I'm honest with them and approachable.

Many have confessed they have never been in this kind of environment. But, by taking this path, my team is fiercely loyal and passionate. They do great work, and it is reflected in the growth of the business.

An effective support system consists of a mix of mentors, colleagues, partners, groups (e.g., mastermind groups, LinkedIn groups), and like-minded organizations.

"You hear horror stories about agency life all the time, unfortunately, and most of us multiple times. To go through hard days, losing a client, someone missing the mark, to know the team is there to support and help you in a constructive way is huge." ~ Ashley

ADVANTAGES OF AN EMPOWERED TEAM

EMPOWERED TEAMS ENHANCE YOUR BUSINESS

You want your team to feel as if they have a voice regarding how the business evolves. It adds to loyalty and increases the likelihood that people will stick around longer. If they feel they're heard and that they can improve the business in a meaningful way, it will lead to lower turnover and attrition.

Hiring and training people is expensive, so keeping them on is better. I am building a business where people want to work here forever. Maybe I'm naïve—I was a revolving door with jobs—but I can guarantee you that we will have a longer lifespan in this company because of the way it's run. We will save money, too, by not constantly hiring and replacing those who left with new hires.

HOW AN EMPOWERED TEAM LEADS TO BUSINESS SUCCESS

They are on the front lines and have access to what's happening day in and day out. When they know their voice matters, they are in a mindset of capturing deficiencies and opportunities, bringing those to the table, and helping the business evolve and get better.

As a business owner, you focus on growing your company; you're not a tactician anymore. In my case, I'm not a social media expert any longer, I'm a social media agency expert. The value I bring is my ability to talk about what we do at a high level and get in front of problems before they become significant. My team looks after me, and I look after the business. My job now is to work *on* the business, not *in* it. I'm in charge of thinking and planning for the business long term … what it will look like and how it will operate six, twelve, eighteen months from now. I trust my team to worry about today.

There are different layers of empowerment: leaders who are empowered to make decisions that don't need to be run by me. They run their teams, and have a sense of ownership, and everyone on the team feels a similar sense of ownership about their work, how they do it, and when they do it.

CHARACTERISTICS OF AN EMPOWERED TEAM

An empowered team is invested in the outcomes of the business. They identify problems and follow up with solutions. They get excited about company growth, are voracious learners, have an entrepreneurial spirit, and always want to get better at what they do.

Empowered team members will often take it upon themselves to remind the rest of the group of the benefits of high productivity, including pay raises and management recognition. They also take on the task of cross-training all the members to do the basics of each other's jobs. This way, if a team member is ever out for some reason, the team can still be productive.

Some other characteristics of an empowered team include:

Focus on the customer or client - Empowered team members put intense focus on ensuring the satisfaction of the customer or client, knowing they pay the bills.

Frontline decision-making - Empowered teams, know they don't have to "ask the boss" before making most decisions. They deal with the day-to-day issues and know what their customers or clients want.

Clear, respectful communication - Teams, like these set clear communication guidelines and expectations that value the input of each member. They also know how to navigate conflict in a healthy way so as not to impede performance.

YOUR ROLE IN TEAM EMPOWERMENT

It starts with hiring people who have those characteristics. And you must be comfortable with letting go. You can't be a control freak. Accept the inherent risks that come with empowerment, knowing that failures and mistakes will happen from time to time. Be confident your team can take care of most of the day-to-day.

That's not easy for many people. Discomfort still exists in me to an extent, but I have to be willing to let go to truly empower the team. Besides, if you hire the right team, the propensity for mistakes will be less, and you can use everything as a learning opportunity. Have a conversation about it—what worked, what didn't, how you would do things differently next time—and move on.

Mistakes in strategy are not really mistakes. Mistakes due to carelessness or lack of effort—that's a performance issue. I'm never going to fault people for taking risks. It's about assessing, learning, and moving forward from there.

Don't get too aggressive with trying new things. There needs to be a certain degree of load-balancing. Empowerment doesn't always mean taking action.

Let your team own service delivery. We have guidelines and a framework for what we do, but they can stray from that if the situation warrants it. Conceptually, it's crucial that they feel they can make decisions.

Collaboration is important. Empowerment isn't doing whatever you want but having the freedom to test ideas.

COMMUNICATING WITH EMPOWERED EMPLOYEES

Communication is critical to everything you do as a digital business. My team and I have developed a relationship where they feel free to challenge me if I am making what, in their view, is a wrong business decision.

I once had a sales call set up with a prospective client, and two of my folks said we needed to change our pitch. They suggested the approach was not as convincing as it could be and that we needed to adjust the way we presented our philosophies. They also said we were giving away too much value up-front without being paid for it and needed to show examples of our work.

Another time, they confronted me about my "sacred cow," our month-to-month contracts. Traditionally, we were a month-to-month agency; I felt that was a way to disrupt. If we do what we say, the client will stay with us.

Their concern was that not having long-term contracts made things more volatile and impeded our growth. They also felt client turnover affected team morale. They would get revved up working with a new client, and the client would leave. Their recommendation: allow clients to opt for either the month-to-month or longer-term contracts for less money. We have ultimately made this shift and most of our clients are trending toward longer-term contracts. I made the final call, but my leadership team helped me get there quicker.

HOW TO EMPOWER YOUR TEAM

Hire the right people. Make their voices heard. Have a direct relationship with all your employees via one-on-ones where you ask questions and get their input. Reward innovation monetarily and in other ways and reinforce that acting in this manner is a core component to advancement in their career. Those are the signals we look for.

Here are some guidelines to follow in empowering your team:

CREATE A SHARED SENSE OF PURPOSE

Making employees feel unified requires that you create and then clearly communicate the organization's purpose. What are the company's core values? What does it stand for? What are your short- and long-term growth goals? Cast a vision and your team will follow your lead.

INVEST IN EMPLOYEE DEVELOPMENT

Foster a culture where continued learning and skill development are rewarded and provide the means for that to happen. Whether that includes funds for education, sending employees to industry conferences, or one-on-one training is up to you. Just make it a priority.

OFFER FEEDBACK REGULARLY

One way to "disempower" your team is to leave them in the dark regarding their performance. That demands regular communication rather than the old-fashioned, fear-inducing formal annual review. Buffer, the social media management platform company, got rid of annual reviews, replacing them with weekly feedback as the best path to foster continuous improvement.[1]

ASK FOR INPUT

You should not only provide feedback but give your team that privilege as well. One surefire way is to ask for their input on critical business decisions. Let them become part of the decision-making process. They will feel valued, and you may find different or better solutions to problems.

Your team is the real star, so finding, hiring, and mentoring are critical components of getting it right. As a business owner, at some point you'll want to transition to working *on* the business and not *in* it, and a world-class team is necessary to feeling comfortable making that transition. It's also going to free you up to do the things a business owner and leader should do to help take the business to the next level.

PART 3

GROWING YOUR
ANTI-AGENCY BUSINESS

CHAPTER TEN

WHY IT'S CRITICAL YOU TREAT YOUR BUSINESS LIKE A CLIENT

The Big Idea: Too many agencies only tell and don't show. Don't be that agency. Treat yourself like a client.

....

Many agencies don't treat themselves like a client. They don't do for themselves what they do for their clients. If you're not doing for yourself what you're suggesting for clients, that's a disconnect that will inhibit business growth.

Whether a prospective client tells you that or not, it factors into their decision-making. If you are too busy servicing your clients to focus on yourself, you won't know about your missed opportunities. Prospects are looking at you, judging you based on what they see, and moving on. Out of sight is out of mind.

We are a social media agency, and many in our industry don't treat themselves like a client. Their efforts aren't a good representation of what they do.

We have had conversations with opportunities we landed that tell us that's why they came to us—we do what we say we do. It is a significant contributing factor in who they decided to work with. If you are a social media agency but your social media sucks, that doesn't send the right signal to prospective clients. You either demonstrate your competency through your brand or miss out on opportunities.

We struggled with this a bit ourselves. We reached a point where I said we are our own client and never take a back seat. It has been a monumental component of our success, resulting in a great deal of validation and many inbound leads based on what we're putting out.

It is a marathon, not a sprint, but the sum of all that effort pays off. You have to keep putting it out, and that's not easy to do. It's much easier to push your stuff to the side. We couldn't allow ourselves to do that. If that means I add more horsepower to our team, that's what we're going to do, I said. That's precisely what we've done.

A mentor of mine said, "Everything Speaks." Everything you put out into the world represents you or your business. Whether it's a blog post, your website, email signature, or what you say in a public environment—all of it contributes to your brand, no matter how insignificant it may seem. You need to be consistent and care about everything you put out into the world.

Conceptually, that's the why; the real meat is the how.

STEPS TO WALKING THE TALK

TREAT YOURSELF AS A CLIENT

Your mindset needs to be to treat your business as you would a client. That includes making sure you assign someone on your team to be responsible for your business. Someone must own that and treat and service your company the same way they would a client. We always have a social media manager on our team assigned to our business as a client and to treat it as such, no different than any of our paid clients. Operationally, it helps us ensure our message doesn't slip through the cracks or get left to the side. If you can't afford that level of investment, hire an external agency to manage it. It may seem crazy to do so, but many businesses fail at taking care of themselves similarly to how they would their clients. And often, it's good to have external perspectives on how to best position yourself.

PULL IN OTHER TEAM MEMBERS

Those in charge of our content creation are the traffic cops pulling things from other team members. That person is not so much doing the work as strategizing and coordinating everyone's efforts. It may come down to a combination of in-house and outsourced providers who do the work.

DECIDE WHICH MEDIA TO USE

Whether it's a blog, podcast, video, or social media, decide the medium(a) that make(s) sense for your target market and resource availability. Don't try to be everything to everybody. Pick the channels and strategies that you can stick to and build off those.

PROVIDE VALUE

Focus on providing value. Be informative and entertaining. Establish an editorial calendar and keyword strategy to guide your efforts. Create content around what you are passionate about and come up with a hit list of themes and topics that relate to your target audience. All your content should have purpose, and that includes value to the reader and value to your business.

OPTIMIZE EVERYTHING

Optimize content for search, so you get found by those looking for what you offer. Everything you put out in the digital world is a signal that helps you get found. Blog posts, social media content, website, podcast ... all of these provide you opportunities to leverage keyword strategies that relate to your business. Optimize this content using the right mix of keywords and phrases that will drive reach and traffic to your website and platforms.

CREATE A CONTENT CALENDAR

You never want to get into a situation of wondering what you are going to post today. Create a content calendar and follow it to the letter. Waiting to figure out what you are going to post for the day is a recipe for failure. Think in advance, and plan out your content a week—ideally a month—in advance.

PUBLISH REGULARLY

We write a blog post every week, put out a podcast every two weeks, and post to social media three times per week. I set aside the same time every Thursday to record my podcast. Get into a rhythm when it comes to publishing. It's the sum of those efforts over time that will deliver the results you're looking for.

Blogging regularly? Might as well put in a few extra steps to increase the likelihood of people finding your posts. If you use WordPress, download the Yoast SEO plugin and follow their prompts on your blog entries to maximize your page optimization.

BONUS TIP: Use Ubersuggest to identify a keyword phrase that is searched for often that relates to your article (and is not overly competitive) and be sure to include it in your blog title, intro paragraph, and in an H1 headline within your post.

ESTABLISH A ROUTINE

Some of the most successful writers and content producers pick the same day and time every week to dedicate to their content creation. If you really want to be consistent with your efforts, find a day and time that works best for you and shut the rest of the world off to focus on producing a week or month's worth of content for your business.

REPURPOSE CONTENT

Not everyone sees your content the first time you publish. Identify and repurpose evergreen content you can regularly share so you don't have to create new content all the time. Do this for a couple of months, and you will have an extensive library of resources to pull from to use on social media, email, and sales pitches. Eventually, you will get to where you only need to create new content one or two times per week.

Everything I have just described is equally important to any business, not just agencies. If you don't have a consistent presence, as people navigate the web to find who to do business with, you become an afterthought.

EVERYTHING SPEAKS

In Chapter Seven, Set Up a Support System, I referenced a former manager and mentor who had a big impact on my life. He said two things that always stood out to me. One was "Don't step over dollars to pick up dimes." And the other, the title of this chapter, "Everything speaks."

THE MEANING OF "EVERYTHING SPEAKS"

Many businesses overlook the importance of their brand and the need to be consistent with how they represent themselves to their audience. What they don't realize is that everything they do as a business matters. Even the seemingly trivial things like an email signature must reflect consistency.

To say "everything speaks" is to suggest that everything you put out in the world matters. Treat everything carefully and make sure it aligns with how you want to present yourself and your perception in the marketplace.

It's the sum of your efforts over an extended period that will add up to success. If you let them slide, inconsistencies can creep in and damage your brand value and reputation. It's a mentality you must reinforce with your team to ensure they share your mindset.

When I started Socialistics, I remember getting excited about the logo and business name and how it was represented visually. It added fuel to my fire. Even our colors are synonymous with our brand. People recognize our name and identity.

APPLYING THE "EVERYTHING SPEAKS" PRINCIPLE

Reinforce the principle with your team as if it's a mantra until they adopt it wholeheartedly, understand the "why," and care about it as much as you do. It doesn't work unless the team is on board, and it starts with the first person you hire.

Applying "everything speaks" means having uniform messaging across the board. It comes down to realizing that you are on stage all the time, and what you do, and every facet, contributes to how other people perceive you.

It also means having your core values and mission statement—the who, what, and why of your business—clearly defined.

It includes your tactics—how you present yourself, your voice, brand guidelines for the visual and written word. Document everything and leave nothing to chance.

Mentor and train new hires about the importance of the "everything speaks" principle and applying it to their work. It must permeate the organization and affect every aspect. That becomes harder as the business grows and you add multiple management layers, but you must maintain it, nonetheless.

Of course, all of this takes time. It goes back to the runway idea I talked about in Chapter Two. Give yourself time to figure that out.

Everything contributes to getting to the point you want—shortcuts and inconsistencies add up that prohibit you from being as successful as you can be. But having these foundational elements in place will help you build a successful business.

WALK THE TALK OUTCOMES

This "walk the talk, don't do as we say, do as we do" mentality offers many benefits and positive outcomes.

The digital landscape is an interesting, changing thing. For the longest time, engagement was the buzzword when it came to measuring the success of digital content. Now, I'm not so sure. Think about your own digital content consuming behavior. Do you like, comment, or share what you consume often? Or do you simply consume and move on? I'm willing to bet that, for most of you, it's the latter. That's true with me as well. You'd be surprised how much of the content you put out in the world actually gets consumed that you don't realize.

Don't let the surface numbers dictate too much when it comes to sticking with your content plan. I can't tell you how many times I've run into people (online and offline) who have made a comment about our podcast, email newsletter, or blog: how they've enjoyed it, find it useful, and so forth. Often, these are people I had no idea were consuming the content. Just because they don't engage, doesn't mean the audience isn't there.

If you lead with providing value, being entertaining, and being informative, and do it consistently, success isn't a matter of if, but when.

For us, it has resulted in a consistent flow of inbound organic leads. It creates authority—we become trusted advisors and subject matter experts. It gives us excellent search visibility, opens opportunities for speaking engagements, and puts us on the map as a recognized social media brand.

Another added benefit of consistently putting out great content is that, inevitably, you'll create resources that you'll be able to leverage in your sales process. After having committed to consistent content over the years, we have a library of resources that we regularly reference in sales calls and inquiries. We can often pull specific podcast episodes or blog posts to reference when they come up in conversations. It's an incredible way to stand out from the crowd and keep your prospects in your sales funnel.

And when you stick with it for a year or more, you're going to position yourself for even bigger and better content opportunities. You'll be able to pull together pieces of content that you've created over the years and develop white papers, e-books, or even something along the lines of what you're reading right now. This book was most definitely pulled from much of the content I've created over the years. Convinced yet of the importance of sticking with your content marketing?

None of this is unique to us. If you start walking the talk and follow through, you'll get there, too. Don't kid yourself, though; it's not easy. It takes much work, commitment, and determination. But if we are an example, it's well worth the effort. Clients see our success, and it becomes a selling point. You can have the same results.

CHAPTER ELEVEN

HOW TO BUILD A SCALABLE LEAD-GENERATING PIPELINE

The Big Idea: Constructing a consistent lead-generating pipeline is a must for any service-based business.

....

If you're in a situation where the only leads you get come from referrals, you won't succeed, not in any significant measure. That approach just doesn't scale. You need an inbound strategy to ensure a consistent flow of leads. You also need a predictable pipeline to forecast what your business needs to thrive and grow.

Building a predictable pipeline starts with your website. Fundamentally, you must have a solid website that includes compelling storytelling and usability so visitors can quickly understand what you do, why, and how you do it. Your website is where they learn what makes you unique.

Once your website is where it needs to be, it's time to go find your customers or clients. There are several ways to create a predictable pipeline, but for us, four stand out: content marketing, paid advertising, sponsorships, and directories. Using these methods, we average twenty to thirty inbound leads from our website alone every month.

CONTENT MARKETING

Getting yourself set up to advertise on Facebook and Google can feel like a daunting task if you don't have any experience with it.

OUR RECOMMENDATION? Start with the "lighter" versions both offer. Run ads through your Google My Business page. On Facebook, do the same through your page admin area. Both scenarios are much more streamlined and easier to set up and manage.

In the previous chapter, we talked about walking the talk around your content plan. Here's where those efforts take shape. Nothing is more valuable to a business than building a pipeline of ad-free leads, but it takes time and commitment.

Once you find the right formula of effective content for your business, produced on a regular basis, over time, you will generate organic website and social media channel traffic that results in business-building leads. You'll start to show up on search results for terms that relate to your business, and you'll find less of a need to spend an exorbitant amount of budget on paid advertising.

PAID ADVERTISING

For many businesses just starting out, the quickest and easiest way to start building a pipeline is investing some budget into paid ads, typically on search or social. The downside is that the pipeline dries up the minute you stop spending. The upside is that, within minutes, you can put yourself in front of a highly targeted audience and start generating traffic and leads to your business.

SPONSORSHIPS

Depending on your type of business, it's likely there are websites or publications specific to your industry and the audience you are trying to reach. These are great places to invest, as the audience relevance increases the potential for a better ROI. Give your business additional exposure by exploring the resources and sponsorship opportunities they offer. Take the time to build a list of organizations, websites, and partners that are likely to have audiences that align with your products and services and explore their sponsorship opportunities.

These can consist of display ads, email newsletters, social media mentions, or paid content opportunities. You'll have to weigh cost, reach potential, and which delivery method makes the most sense with what you are promoting. Typically, we lean more toward paid content opportunities ... something with a little more depth that can pull people in, but pairing those with top-of-the-funnel ad opportunities like display ads can be a great combo to generate traffic.

BUSINESS DIRECTORIES

Once you begin producing great content and putting it out regularly, get your business listed on industry-related directories. For us, that includes sites such as Clutch, UpCity, and The Manifest—directories with tremendous search visibility. We get a ton of leads from them.

Directories are investing hundreds of thousands of dollars in getting on Google's front page for what you do, so piggyback on those efforts. Don't try to compete with them; partner with them instead.

The best way to find directories related to your business or industry is to do keyword searches on Google. Identify five or ten of the top keywords for your business or industry, conduct a search, see which

Everything referenced in this chapter takes time and patience—time your business may not have, particularly when you are just getting started. Ways to build a predictable pipeline more quickly include paid social and search campaigns and industry organization and event sponsorships.

directories appear on the front page of results, and get listed in them. Usually, it's free to simply be listed, so this is your first step.

Create a detailed profile, share your portfolio or examples of work, and optimize the listing for search. You may also want to inquire about sponsorship to increase visibility. Up to 20 percent of your pipeline can come from this.

Most important? Reviews. We'll dive into this later, but prioritizing getting your clients or customers to leave you reviews, especially on these directory listings, is the most critical component of ranking higher and pushing prospects to contact you.

Directories will pull people in, but once a prospect or searcher gets to your site, they need content that builds trust. When they come to your site and see little or no content, they will move on. Without the content component in your marketing strategy, directories won't do you nearly as much good.

BUILD CUSTOM LANDING PAGES FOR AD CAMPAIGNS

If you decide to advertise, have a custom landing page tied to each ad that contains the same content. The landing page must reinforce the same keywords, topic, and content as shown in the ad. Whatever you do, don't send them to the home page of your website. This is the easy way out and not the best use of your advertising budget. You need to direct paid traffic to a customized experience that reinforces the message they get from your paid ads, and this is accomplished through custom landing pages.

One element every landing page needs is a clear call to action. If you're selling a product, tie it to a promotion. If it's services you provide, offer a free consultation, newsletter sign-up, or downloadable resource in exchange for their name and email address—anything to provoke an action.

We've developed some incredible tools that were born from these efforts, including a social media ad budget calculator and a social media report card. Both are tools that prospects can access free of charge that drive interest and build our prospect lists. They took little effort to develop but provide tremendous value to a wide audience. Chances are there are similar tools in your business that you can identify and develop that will do the same.

You also need a CRM (customer relationship management) tied to the page to capture and house all the leads. Once you start driving a decent amount of traffic and leads, it becomes unsustainable to try and "wing it." You'll need technology to help keep your pipeline organized and easy to manage. There are various options available to fit every budget, from Mailchimp, which is free up to a point but limited in its capabilities, all the way to enterprise tools like Salesforce and HubSpot.

We use a CRM called Pipedrive at Socialistics. It helps us see clearly and efficiently what's going on with each of the leads we receive. We love it for its ease of use and focus strictly on helping you manage your pipeline.

CREATE EMAIL SEQUENCES

Once you have a pipeline in place, you need a scalable way to communicate with it. Typically, your pipeline will consist of a variety of prospects that range from "hot" to "cold" and everything in between. Over time you will determine how you categorize these opportunities and what process you put in place to service them.

Regardless, there is going to be a high percentage of opportunities that aren't quite ready for you yet but that you want to stay in touch with. You never know when a "no" can be turned into a "yes," and that will only happen if you stay top of mind with cold prospects. This is where automation comes into play and building out an established sequence of prewritten emails. There will be categories of prospects that may not require a personalized one-to-one approach, but hitting them with prewritten, relevant messaging that nurtures them toward that is the goal. Throw those who are not a yes into a weekly or monthly newsletter sequence. (More on this later.)

JUST SAY NO TO AWARD "SHOWS"

If you already own an agency, you've probably received an email like this:

"I am glad to inform you that we have shortlisted your company as one of the most valuable companies in the '50 Most Valuable Brands of the Year' list. It will be two full-page in-depth features about your company's differentiators, products, services, challenges, road map,

*and how the CEO is driving the company with an interesting photograph
and heading. We will also talk about how all 50 valuable brands are giving
their best to the business community and their effort toward the ecosystem."*

–Unnamed Questionable Publication

This is just one example of an email I've received in the past "congratulat-
ing" me for being "prequalified" or "shortlisted" as a prestigious award-winner
for the "insert clever name here" award or honor. There is a growing trend for
this practice and it's pretty simple … and quite clever, honestly.

It basically works like this:

1. These companies or organizations build up a following or audience
   and leverage that to create either an event or offering designed to
   drive revenue.
2. They target small or upcoming marketing agencies that covet being an
   "award-winner" to help drive their business.
3. They use tactics and language to make you feel like you are part of an
   exclusive group and that you're eligible for the award by simply replying
   that you're interested.
4. This is usually followed by an "interview" or "selection stage," which is
   nothing other than a period they predetermine is long enough to make
   you feel like there is some sort of process involved. There isn't.
5. You get contacted later with a congratulatory email saying YOU'VE
   BEEN SELECTED! That's followed by some nonsensical process
   about how you "won."
6. You then are instructed to fill out whatever forms and simply pay their
   substantial event, registration, or advertising package fees.

Many agencies that know there is no substance to these awards just want
to slap a badge on their website or send out a press release. The fact of the
matter is most potential clients won't know or take the time to vet these
claims. The agencies are pretty much paying for the "awards" or "accolades"
and don't care that they hold no real weight.

The truth is, I almost pulled the trigger myself for our agency along the way. I actually followed through to see how it would play out. It was tempting, but at the end of the day, I couldn't do it because it flies in the face of one of our core values: authenticity. Even though most of our competition does it, we made the decision that we wouldn't. We'll stick with our work speaking for itself and winning awards that are truly earned.

There are, of course, legitimate awards that aren't too difficult to identify. Two of the more well-known in the advertising and marketing world are the Clios and Ad Age. Typically, legit operations are much more difficult to win and involve an established vetting process that requires diving into the actual work you've done. Find the "real" ones in your industry (usually one or two) and focus on those. What's the best barometer to know if they are legit? They won't contact you. You have to contact them.

Bottom line, if it doesn't feel right (and most of them won't), walk away.

Remember, you can't treat marketing and a pipeline like a light switch—on one day and off the next. It's the sum of those efforts that creates opportunity. The more visible you are on search and social, the better. You never know when or where an opportunity may present itself.

CHAPTER TWELVE

ONE STRATEGY TO IMPLEMENT IMMEDIATELY

The Big Idea: Podcasting has become popular again and is an excellent strategy to grow your business. It can help you gain visibility, build trust, and grow influence with customers and colleagues. Give it a try.

....

Podcasts are exploding in popularity, and they are not going away anytime soon. That's why I'm calling them out as a means to grow your business.

Those who have never done it think of podcasting as a monumental task, like producing a television or radio show. I have been podcasting for more than a year and learned how to do it in a scalable way. It's relatively easy to pull off and not as sophisticated as you might think. This chapter demystifies the process by addressing the challenges and outlining the advantages to make it manageable and scalable.

MY PODCAST STORY

I started a podcast for personal reasons: my love of baseball. Having played (and still do), a friend and I started Comebacker, a podcast covering adult baseball. It was a way to dip my toe in the water and get a sense of how podcasting works. It allowed me to learn and play around.

When I shifted to using a podcast for our agency, I didn't think of it as a business development tool but more of a way to talk about what we're doing, tell stories about our experience, and help others. I felt I was doing it for the right reasons with the right motives in mind, and it grew from there.

For me, it was therapeutic. I was not around other people much, having practically launched our business during a pandemic. Podcasting was a way to talk about my experiences and have weekly conversations with folks I would never have met or known in person. Somewhat to my surprise, business relationships have come out of it. I use it to grow the business in a variety of ways. It fuels our blog and complements what we do across the board.

One of my favorite episode types is interviewing some of our current clients. Assuming you take great care in servicing yours, it's a tremendous way to build your reputation (more on that later) and can be a great sales tool to attract similar types of businesses. Early in our podcast days, we interviewed one of our favorite clients, a collaborative law attorney. After publishing our episode, we got more downloads and usage out of that one episode than all our others previously. Not to mention it opened new opportunities for us with similar businesses across the US.

ADVANTAGES TO PODCASTING FOR BUSINESS

There are numerous advantages to using podcasting to promote your business.

Your audience and prospects look at having a podcast through a more celebrity-ish lens: "Oh, you have a podcast." They think of it like it's a TV show. It adds a layer of social proof and credibility that you might not get otherwise. It offers educational and entertainment value. You can use it to provide tips and helpful information to the listener.

It's a lead-generation source. Something I do is invite decision-makers from my prospect list as a guest to talk about their business. I tell them that we have a podcast, have learned about their business, and want to invite them to come on and talk about it. It's a far easier way to get their attention than a sales call. I use it as an opportunity to get to know them and build a relationship that could lead to a business relationship in the future.

A podcast is also a great sales tool. As you develop an inventory, you can use them in sales calls, referencing a particular episode as a resource. Over time, you'll have a library of episodes that you can pull from that will eventually cover just about any subject that's relevant.

Last, a podcast is not as challenging to produce as you might think. There are efficiencies around talking rather than having to write. More people are more comfortable talking about things than writing. Plus, the demand and popularity are high. It's something every business should seriously consider.

ADVANTAGES FOR THE LISTENER

For listeners, podcasting is one of the most accessible forms of communication. People can take it on the go and listen while on a walk, exercising, or driving. They can have it on in the background. Unlike video or reading, it doesn't require 100 percent of someone's attention. It's a low-commitment form of content that is incredibly portable. In addition, most podcast episodes tend to contain evergreen content. To this day, many of our older podcast episodes are still consumed on a regular basis.

PODCASTING CHALLENGES

You need to be comfortable being a "performer." Good interviewing takes skill and preparation. You have to be a good conversationalist and make conversations about them and not you. It must be something you enjoy. Otherwise, it won't work. You need to take the time to research guests and be prepared to demonstrate you've done your homework with them to get the most out of these conversations.

Podcasting takes time to learn, but not as much as you may think. Do some research regarding the equipment and software you need. There are also upfront setup costs, though they don't have to be expensive. I recommend getting help from someone who knows how to do podcasting. Let them do the editing and tech work, so you can focus on recording, finding guests, and producing the show.

Finding guests for your podcast shouldn't be too difficult, but vetting them can be. Not everyone is going to be a good fit, regardless of what their press kit might look like.

BONUS TIP: Create a landing page form asking your potential guests a series of questions to help you vet them like a pro. That way you can make sure you avoid the dreaded "awful guest" experience.

NEED SOME INSPIRATION? Check out ours at https:// socialistics.com/podcast-guest-questionnaire/.

WHAT MAKES A GOOD PODCAST?

Central Theme. Your podcast must cater to a specific audience, and you need to stick with a central theme. Don't try to be everything to everybody; there's an audience for practically everything. Pick what makes the most sense for your business and what you're passionate about and stick with it. This goes for episodes as well.

Regular Schedule. Stick to a regular schedule for your podcast. For most starting out, I recommend every other week or once a month to get into a rhythm. If you really enjoy it and have the content to support it, every week is ideal.

Structure. Make sure your episodes follow a set structure. Perhaps you prerecord intros? Mid-show ad rolls? Intro/outro music? Figure out how you want to lay out your show and stick with it.

Compelling Content. Whether it's just you, or you have a guest, the content must be great, otherwise, what's the point? Don't do it just to do it—make every episode count. Share stories, bring on interesting guests who have something valuable to share. Always think ahead enough to make sure your episodes matter.

Behind the Scenes. A great podcast has the bones to ensure it has staying power. Make sure you're incorporating sound SEO strategies with your podcast through your descriptions, transcriptions, and how you market it across social media and the web. You want people to find your podcast; if they don't, why bother?

HOW TO START A PODCAST

Start with strategy. You will need to create an editorial strategy and content calendar consisting of themes and topics to talk about. Create a list of topic ideas, people you'd like to interview. Get your list at least twenty-five ideas deep.

Decide on the medium. Whether you do audio only or add video depends on what you're comfortable with. Video requires more production value and goes back to attention span. You need 100 percent of the viewer's attention. For most folks, starting out with just audio is the way to go. Get your bearings and establish a regular rhythm before committing to adding video.

Equip yourself. Don't get overwhelmed trying to find overly expensive equipment. You'll do fine with a sub-$100 microphone. Pair it with a stand/arm, shock mount, and filter, and you're ready to go. There are hundreds of articles on the web that can point you in the right direction on an affordable setup.

Find people to interview. This isn't difficult, but it does take time. Sites like PodcastGuest.com, Podchaser, and MatchMaker.fm are good places to start to look for guests. Also, search for people in your network and prospect list. In time, people will start reaching out to you.

Make time for recording. Carve out a regular time slot—the same time every week—to record episodes. Once you get into a rhythm, it will become natural. Use a scheduling tool like Calendly to create an accessible booking link with the times you set aside for guests to easily schedule with you.

Regarding recording, there are several tools out there that can help you with recording your episodes. Two platforms we have used that are our favorites are Squadcast (https://squadcast.fm/) and ECamm Live (https://www.ecamm.com/). Both are affordable and will meet your needs, so it comes down to personal preference.

Most folks don't have experience editing audio or video. For them, I strongly recommend budgeting for this unless you're passionate about learning. If so, the go-to software is Garageband on the Mac and Audicity on PC, both free options. Otherwise, do a simple web search for podcast editing and you'll find tons of options to help you take care of the technical side of things.

One of the oft-overlooked strategies for podcast episodes is making sure you develop written transcripts of your episodes. However, who wants that job? Not you. Once your episodes are published, go to Fiverr.com and find someone who specializes in podcast transcriptions. With a little effort, you'll uncover cheap, affordable options to provide you with accurate and ready-to-publish transcripts that you can add to your episodes and, more importantly, for your blog posts!

Hosting. You'll need a place where your podcast episodes will actually live. Similar to your website, there are a number of affordable options for this. We recommend Buzzsprout (https://www.buzzsprout.com/) or Anchor (https://anchor.fm/). They'll take care of all the heavy lifting and help you get your podcast on all the major listening platforms.

Market the podcast. Talk about it on social channels, share it in groups, get it in front of people you want to listen to it. Your guests will share it with their audiences as well. Turn your podcast episodes into blog posts.

Don't be fooled by the perceived complexities of launching and maintaining a podcast. Once you get the right tools and processes in place, you'll find it to be one of the most productive and successful content marketing strategies you can incorporate into your business. And, for most people, one of the more enjoyable parts of being a business owner.

Building a predictable pipeline starts with your website. Fundamentally, you must have a solid website that includes compelling storytelling and usability, so visitors can quickly understand what you do, why, and how you do it. Your website is where they learn what makes you unique.

Once your website is where it needs to be, it's time to go find your customers or clients. There are several ways to create a predictable pipeline.

CHAPTER THIRTEEN

HOW NEWER OR SMALLER AGENCIES CAN FIND AND WIN BIGGER DEALS

The Big Idea: The best clients are the ones who have healthy budgets but who no one has heard of. Here's how to find them.

....

Don't go after the Apples or Microsofts of the world when you're just starting out—you're not going to get them unless you know someone on the inside well. Instead, you want to go after the brands that are similar in size, but that most people have never heard of. I call them the "Big Nobodies."

One of the biggest clients we landed in our early days was a brand you have probably never heard of but was close to a being a billion-dollar company. Even though we were only a small upstart boutique agency, we were able to land a piece of their business that would not only be a high-paying, profitable client, but also give us the experience and portfolio piece that would help us grow as an agency.

So why did they hire us and not someone bigger and/or more experienced? It all comes down to how you present yourself and having the confidence to turn any of your perceived weaknesses into strengths.

When you're starting out, it can be intimidating and daunting to go after bigger companies with the thought being, "Why would they hire a little outfit like us?" You've got to change your mindset when it comes to what you bring to the table, even at this early stage. For the longest time, I was convinced I had to make my agency look bigger than it was to compete with larger agencies. I'd think to myself, "How in the world can I compete with these bigger established agencies for business?" The truth was, and is, that being small can be an incredible advantage. When you're smaller, you can be more nimble, more attentive to your client's needs. You're not overly established in your processes, and you're probably much hungrier for the opportunity. Those are strengths, and they can differentiate you in the marketplace.

The key is to turn your perceived weaknesses into strengths and to embrace who you are and what you have to offer. The truth is, many larger companies prefer working with smaller businesses or agencies and the value that can come with that. Don't discount your competitive advantage versus bigger competition. Once we embraced our "smallness," we started to land more business.

WHAT IS A BIG NOBODY CLIENT?

A Big Nobody client is a multimillion-dollar or more business that has some history and is successful but isn't well known outside their industry. Typically, they are niche, catering to a smaller segment of the population. Often, they are B2B companies versus direct to consumers.

They have the budget and can afford to pay an agency to do their marketing. They know they have a need and don't stress spending the dollars to meet it. Bottom line: They need you and they have the means to pay for it.

ADVANTAGES OF BIG NOBODY CLIENTS

One advantage to finding these big nobodies is that, chances are, you're not going to compete with a ton of other agencies. The fact that they are not as well known means they can fall under the radar and are ripe for opportunity. Also, decision-makers can be more accessible and easier to find as opposed to large enterprises. You can use tools like Seamless or ZoomInfo to find their contact information. There may not be as many layers of bureaucracy, red tape, or multiple decision-makers to satisfy either.

SOME EXAMPLES OF BIG NOBODY CLIENTS

What niche or niches does your business serve? Let's say you focus on insurance. Well, everyone knows State Farm, Geico, AllState … how's about Trupanion? They're one of the biggest pet insurance companies in the world.

Or perhaps you target technology or software companies? Of course, everyone knows Microsoft, Google, Facebook … and sure, carving out a piece of business in those places would be amazing, but it's tough to break through those walls if you don't have any existing relationships with folks inside. How's about Remitr, a fast-growing fintech company out of Toronto, or PointClickCare, a burgeoning cloud-based tech provider for the senior care industry? With a little homework, you can quickly find companies nobody has heard of but that have deep pockets and need your help.

HOW TO FIND BIG NOBODY CLIENTS

Even though these sorts of clients aren't household names, it doesn't mean they are that difficult to find. What it really comes down to is having the right approach and narrowing your search by industry.

If you are a service-based business, look at your portfolio and find industries that stand out. You are much more likely to attract decision-makers' attention if you can lead with work or products and services that cater specifically to their industry.

Once you've identified an industry or two, then you're ready to start your detective work.

WAYS TO FIND THEM

Here are some tools and steps to follow when searching for big nobody clients.

Crunchbase is a platform for finding business information about private and public companies, many of which are newer and have been through at least one funding round. They have money to spend, much of which can go to marketing. Regarding reaching decision-makers, Crunchbase provides contact information to C-suite members.

Seamless.ai is an affordable artificial intelligence platform that enables you to extract contact data from websites and LinkedIn profiles. It's like ZoomInfo but much less expensive.

Hunter.io is a Chrome extension that offers a free version, which enables you to find contact info from websites quickly. It is a great first tool to use when you're starting out.

Search industry-related terms in your state. Go a couple of pages deep. These companies don't typically have front-page visibility and can likely use more help. Dig a bit, and then use Seamless to find the contact info for decision-makers.

Subscribe to LinkedIn Sales Navigator, a search tool for salespeople to find decision-makers and executives. You can search using a variety of criteria, including industry.

Build a prospect list. Combine manual research and these tools to build prospect lists, then reach out via a one-on-one introductory email. You get bonus points for having examples of work you've done in that industry.

List Searches: Do a search for "top (insert your industry here) in (insert year here)" on Google and browse the variety of articles that showcase up-coming companies in your niche or industry.

WAYS THEY CAN FIND YOU

Search. Google search is one way these big nobodies will find you. If you have worked in a particular industry, create a landing page containing content specific to it. Conduct research into often-searched terms that have a high probability of intent around what you do. Bake these into your content, so you show up in search.

Did you have to work a little to find a prospect? Good. Use that experience as a sales strategy when reaching out. If you had to work to find them, chances are their prospects will too, and that's where you come in.

Events. Find the tradeshows, events, and organizations specific to the industry of the companies you want to work with. Become a member, offer content, and position yourself to speak at these events to increase your profile and get in front of decision-makers.

Referrals and Word of Mouth. Another, even better way they will find you is through referrals and word of mouth. Ninety percent of the business we get searches us out, not the other way around.

HOW TO PREPARE FOR THE BIG NOBODY CLIENTS

The separation is in the preparation. If you want to stand out, you need to do your homework. The reality is, you're going to have to work a little harder and put more time into winning new business than your bigger competition.

If you take nothing else away from this chapter, take this ... follow the 3 P's and you'll find yourself winning opportunities that your bigger brothers and sisters aren't.

PREPARATION

Put in the time to get to know your prospects. Who are they, who do they compete with, what opportunities do they have? What problems do they face? Arm yourself with a wealth of knowledge before approaching your prospects, and you'll be ten times more likely to get a response from them rather than dying in their inbox.

PASSION

Whenever I'm asked what's the one thing that separates our agency from others when it comes to winning business, it's simple: PASSION! Yeah, it sounds corny, but trust me, it isn't. It's really hard to fake passion day in and day out. You need to feel and show your passion in what you do and who you do it for. When I'm authentically passionate for an opportunity and it shows, we typically land 90 percent or more of those opportunities. Takeaway? Only go after opportunities you're authentically passionate about, and bring high energy when you do.

PERSISTENCE

Don't give up. Most sales statistics and articles say it takes at least six to eight touch points on average to get a response. Don't be naïve and think your well-crafted initial email will get the job done. The reality is, you don't know when, where, or how people are working at any given time, and sometimes people are just busy. I can think of plenty of times I ignored multiple attempts at getting my attention only to eventually get hit at the right time. Don't give up, and be persistent in your pursuit of new opportunities. Especially if they are worth it.

Don't always settle for the low-hanging fruit opportunities. There are big pieces of business to be won. With a little extra planning, effort, and execution, you can land them and help propel your business faster than you can imagine. Chances are, you are as much of a nobody to these prospective clients as they are to you, so put in the work, employ the 3 P's, and you'll find yourself winning some big opportunities that can propel your business.

Remember, success breeds success.

CHAPTER FOURTEEN

FORGET COLD OUTREACH. WHY GOING WARM IS THE WAY TO GO

The Big Idea: Cold email just plain isn't worth the slog. Your time is better spent building warm email strategies.

....

In the last chapter, "Find the Big Nobodies," I talked about the use of one-to-one introductory emails. In this chapter, I recommend not using cold emails. I know, it sounds like a contradiction.

I'm referring to not creating cold email broadcasts—one message sent to hundreds or thousands of people who have never heard of you—names you got from a purchased list, for example. That's different from personalized one-to-one communication. It is a spray-and-pray, one-to-many, scattershot approach that, in my opinion, is not the best use of your time or resources.

Times have changed, and more and more people are growing weary of unsolicited communication. Short attention spans have taken over, and there is too much digital content to rifle through for most people. Unsolicited mass communication is typically incredibly ineffective and can do more harm than good.

WHY COLD EMAILS AREN'T WORTH THE TROUBLE

The number one reason not to use cold email broadcasts is that people are protective of their inboxes. They don't like getting mass emails from businesses they don't know or have not opted to receive info from.

They ignore them. Delete them. Unsubscribe from them. Or report them. In their minds, it's spam. And if you haven't gotten their permission to communicate with them, technically it is.

And most mass email sending platforms don't like you to send emails from purchased lists—many straight-up prohibit it. Plus, the success rate is minimal considering the amount of time and money you put in—resources that could be better spent on more effective strategies.

If you asked one hundred people if they want to get mass email in their inbox, I'm willing to bet the majority would say absolutely not and would prefer their inboxes are filled with communication from those they know, or, at the very least, contains information specific to them.

Statistics bear that out: One study found that the average cold email response rate was 1 percent,[1] which means for every one hundred people you email, you're getting through to one person (and bothering the rest).

So, if ninety-nine don't want it, why continue doing it?

Admittedly, this has the potential for debate. There are those with strong opinions who stand in defense of the tactic. I'm not saying it can't work, but that's the exception rather than the rule. And, as a business owner, you must prioritize your time and resources. You have to make hard decisions on where to spend the resources you have, and there are better ways to do so as a newer business. To me, doing this just doesn't make sense.

You can't do this and all the other things I have talked about in this book. Maybe once you have a sales team, then integrating this might make sense. But when you're starting out, it's not the best use of time and money.

A BETTER WAY

There is a better way to approach email marketing: warm emails where people opt in to receive them. Or, at the very least, slightly warm.

My advice: Build your own list from your content marketing and advertising efforts. You ask their permission, and they consent. Then, you focus on providing value without any other intent. Be helpful, interesting, putting out information people want to consume. Open rates will increase, and spam complaints will go way down.

According to Campaign Monitor, an email marketing platform, you should expect open rates to be 15–25 percent on average, click-through rates as high as 2.5 percent, and click-to-open rates between 20 and 30 percent.[2] That's much better than the 1 percent from cold email, wouldn't you agree?

Our list has grown to about 1,000 now and consists only of people who have expressly opted in through free downloads, subscribing on our website, or reaching out to us for more information. It's not a get-rich-quick scheme. It takes time to build a list, but it is much more effective long term.

Because you never know when someone is ready to do business with you, it helps you stay top of mind, so when they are ready, they think of you. If you're in their world regularly, it's you they will call when the time comes. This happens fairly regularly with us.

We've had clients who have either worked with us previously and had to stop for a variety of reasons and ones who opted to go with someone else but then reengaged with us. Why? Because we remained top of mind by regularly sending them insightful tips, advice, and updates on our business.

HOW TO CREATE A WARM EMAIL CAMPAIGN

Create valuable content in various forms—a blog, email newsletter, social media posts, podcasts. Talk about what you do; provide tips and helpful ideas, but don't be overly salesy. This is not about selling but providing value, so don't go in hot with buy, buy, buy. That's one sure way to turn list members off, and many will unsubscribe. This is about the long game—building relationships and trust with people who aren't ready to buy but will be over time.

Use an email sending platform, such as Mailchimp or Active Campaign, and some sort of CRM, like Pipedrive or HubSpot. There are plenty of affordable tools available to help you publish content, capture emails, and track activity.

Regarding frequency, I advise no more than one email per week. How often you mail depends on what you have going on that can be repurposed for use. We have enough fuel to pull from to support this level of activity.

NOT ENTIRELY CONVINCED? HOW ABOUT LUKEWARM EMAIL?

I know what you're thinking ... I don't have time to build out a list. I need results now! Or perhaps the prospect of sending out 500 emails at the click of a button is too enticing? Well, I still recommend avoiding the latter, but here's another method to consider. Do your research and narrow down to a more manageable list of say twenty or thirty. Do your homework on each. Who are they? Where is the opportunity? Where can you make a difference for them specifically?

Take your lukewarm outreach even further by pairing it with a custom landing page that speaks specifically to the industry you're targeting. And include a freebie, such as an ebook, webinar, or some free value-add that has the ability of turning that lukewarm prospect into a hot one!

Carve out two hours every week to build a lukewarm list of cold prospects and reach out with personalized messaging specific to them. Yes, technically it's cold outreach, but it won't come off that way if you take a bit of time and personalize each message—an approach that's somewhere in the middle between traditional cold outreach and warm inbound. It's the approach we take, and it comes with a much higher success rate. Even better, use a tool like Loomly to record a personal video taking them through a screen share of something specific you think you can help them with. A few extra minutes in effort can go a long way in getting a response.

The amount of time, effort, and resources you pour into cold email isn't worth the slog.

I tried doing this on five different occasions, hiring different companies, and it never worked. I did get one client, but the amount of time and expense wasn't worth it. It's much better to use warm email strategies to reach people who want to hear from you.

People have short attention spans. They are inundated with social media, email, and text—it's become all noise. Be interesting and valuable, stand out, and demonstrate some personalization in your outreach. The added time will be offset by the higher response rates.

CHAPTER FIFTEEN

WHY PRIORITIZING YOUR ONLINE REPUTATION IS A MUST

The Big Idea: Demand for your business is driven by the quality of your reputation. Live and breathe your values to create a positive brand image.

....

The internet has enabled people to publish information about themselves and publicly comment on others' in a readily accessible manner. The fact that we can easily read, see, or hear what other people have to say is one of the key features of internet-enabled communication.

Social media expert Brian Solis said, "Welcome to a new era of marketing and service in which your brand is defined by those who experience it."

What he means is that your online reputation is not determined by what you say about yourself as a company so much as it is by what others say about you. That's why it's so important to stick with your core values and be true to who you are to create as positive a brand reputation as possible.

When people type your company's products, services, or name into Google, a list of reviews shows up. The same is true for sites like Facebook and Yelp. Prospective customers will look comparatively between brand pages that compete for the same keywords and often make their purchase decision based on the number and quality of customer reviews.

For those reasons, your business needs to build and manage its online reputation. Your brand's reputation matters. It can hit revenues and, if negative, can cripple or even kill your company.

Don't believe me? Maybe these statistics[1] will convince you.

- 97 percent of prospective customers read online reviews to find a local business.
- 74 percent of prospects who see customer reviews on a business's website state that they would contact that business.
- 49 percent of potential customers say a business needs to have at least a four-star rating before considering it.
- 30 percent of prospective customers say that they judge a business positively when it responds to its customers' online reviews.
- 87 percent compare businesses while they shop online.
- 83 percent of potential customers trust recommendations from online users as opposed to advertising.
- 78 percent of potential customers trust peer recommendations; only 14 percent of potential customers trust advertising.
- Four in five people claim that they have received advice through social media on what product or service to purchase.
- 56 percent of potential customers have found information that convinced them to purchase from a business or individual.
- 89 percent of online shoppers have stopped using online services and purchasing from businesses because they have experienced poor customer support.
- 70 percent of complaining customers are willing to do business with a company again if their complaint is resolved in their favor.

- 39 percent of Facebook users like brand pages to see and get information on different products.
- 94 percent of potential customers only look at the first page of Google results.
- 56 percent of potential customers don't think about the consequences of their online activities.
- 61 percent of potential customers have a higher opinion of brands when they offer a good mobile experience.

ONLINE REPUTATION BENEFITS

If those statistics prove anything, it's that every business, regardless of industry, must monitor what's being said about it online.

Managing your reputation offers several benefits:

Increases Sales. Before deciding to purchase a product or service, consumers tend to search online. And before they buy from a particular brand, they read online reviews to see what people say about the brand and its products and services.

Maintains Transparency. Visibility on the internet is critical and enhanced through a well-designed and content-rich website or company blog.

Builds Trust. People tend to buy from brands they know, like, and trust. Trust is the currency of the digital economy.

Improves Brand Image. An effective online reputation management strategy can assist businesses when it comes to building their brand image. By regularly monitoring the responses on their communication channels, companies can create the brand image they want.

Collects Insights. Smart companies use customer reviews as feedback to improve their products and services.

THE BIG THREE: GOOGLE, FACEBOOK, AND YELP

Now that you see the importance of building your company's reputation online, where do you start? I recommend the "Big Three": Google (search), Facebook (social media), and Yelp (customer reviews).

GOOGLE

Google accounts for 64 percent of the world's reviews.[2] The best way to control your online reputation on Google is by applying solid search engine optimization knowledge that includes:

High-quality content that directly addresses your audience's problems and hardships.

Establishing an active presence on social media, Google, blogs, YouTube, and image sites. Ensure that you update all your accounts with relevant news, images, and articles representing your business.

Owning a fully optimized Google My Business profile where you monitor and respond to reviews consistently. Not only will this increase your visibility in location-based searches, but it also increases the probability of you appearing on Google Local Pack. (Reviews are the second most powerful ranking factor in Google's Local Pack.[3])

Ranking your business on Google Local Pack also improves your local SEO, which can boost your website's traffic and lead to more sales, store visits, or any call to action on your website.

If you prioritize anything when it comes to building your online reputation through reviews, start here. It has the biggest impact on your ability to be more easily found and is the most accessible window into what your clients and customers can say about you.

FACEBOOK

Facebook is the world's largest social network, with 3.2 billion monthly active users (including users on Facebook-owned services like WhatsApp, Messenger, and Instagram).[4]

Two in three users visit a Facebook business page at least once a week. Moreover, one in three people uses the platform to look for Facebook reviews and recommendations. More than 50 percent of consumers consider Facebook to be the most common place to learn about new brands and products. And 66 percent are likely to share their thoughts, experiences, and opinions on their purchases.

Most businesses create a Facebook page where customers can leave reviews and indicate a star rating prominently displayed on the page and search.

With most social media users on Facebook, getting reviews on your Facebook business page should be a crucial part of your review monitoring process. Like Google reviews, Facebook reviews can accommodate any business from any industry. There's no reason it shouldn't be within your review management scope.

Facebook updated its platform not long ago and now calls reviews "Recommendations." With Recommendations, your customers can rate your business simply by choosing whether they recommend it.

Enabling Recommendations on your business page is a crucial Facebook reputation management tactic. Doing so demonstrates your company's willingness to receive and listen to valuable customer feedback. Reviews and recommendations also help prospective customers learn more about your business from actual customers and make your brand easier to find in Facebook search results.

Other tactics you should make part of your Facebook marketing strategy include:

A recognizable Facebook profile picture

Branding matters. Being recognized helps people to find your profile and like and follow it. Your profile picture is used as a thumbnail for all your posts, so choose wisely by using your logo or an image that instantly connects users to your brand.

A compelling company profile

The "About" section is one of the first places people will look when scanning your company Facebook page. Ensure yours displays relevant company information—and a compelling story.

Engaging people with posts

Add post content, graphics, videos, and more to your page to engage your followers. HubSpot says that companies with less than 10,000 followers receive 60 percent fewer interactions when they post over sixty times per month.[5]

You don't need to overdo it—too much will put people off. Spend time thinking about what your followers want to see, what they need, and what they like. Facebook Insights will help you understand what type of posts get better engagement and reach. Use what it reveals to craft similar posts in the future.

Quick responses

When your followers comment, ask questions, or offer praise (or even negative reviews), take the time to respond—and do so quickly. Quick responses provide the speed and convenience people crave and present a brand that customers can rely on when there's an issue. Implement social media guidelines across your business and determine how you want to respond and in what time frame.

YELP

Yelp is an interactive customer review platform that allows users to express their views about a business by writing reviews. At the time of this writing, the site had more than 224 million reviews worldwide, making it the largest site of its kind on the planet.[6] That means you'd better not underestimate its value in the eyes of the consumer. Even a one-star improvement in your rating can lead to between a 5 and 9 percent increase in revenue.[7]

Also, a Nielsen study commissioned by Yelp revealed that 92 percent of users purchase after visiting the platform.[8] Talk about the importance of word-of-mouth marketing!

Yelp doesn't necessarily make sense for all businesses, though. It's really geared more toward the consumer market: home services, restaurants, entertainment, etc. If you offer B2B services, then you probably don't need to concern yourself too much with it.

NICHE INDUSTRY DIRECTORIES & REVIEW SITES

Another way to build and maintain your online reputation is to identify and get listed in industry-specific niche directories and review sites with front-page search visibility. It doesn't matter what industry your business is in either; there's a directory for you.

For example, as a marketing agency, Socialistics is listed in Clutch (clutch. co) and UpCity (upcity.com), and B2B business directories. SaaS companies would want a listing in G2.

Be very selective about where you list your business, however. Many directories, to put it frankly, aren't worth your time. Often, their monthly traffic is small, and they have minimal domain authority with Google. You want the ones that have front-page visibility. They are spending a tremendous amount of money and resources to get that front-page real estate, and you're not going to be able to compete with that. Take advantage of the work they're doing and piggyback by making sure you're listed and considering their paid ad opportunities.

BUSINESS DIRECTORY LISTING BENEFITS

There are several benefits you can accrue by getting listed. Two, in particular, come to mind. A business listing helps you:

Amplify your online presence. Business directories spend lots of money to get front-page Google returns. Don't compete. Partner with them instead.

Build your brand profile. Business directory listings can help strengthen your brand profile. Directories can contain more than just your business name, address, and phone number (referred to as the "NAP") and can also carry your social media links, photos and videos, customer feedback, and promotions.

IDENTIFY AFFORDABLE SPONSORSHIP OPPORTUNITIES

Business directory sponsorships increase brand awareness even further by promoting your listing at or near the top of the page. Directories will often highlight your listing with bigger and bolder type, colors, and more features than unpaid listings offer.

Your business gets greater visibility, more attention, and more implicit trust by having a sponsored listing. Think of it as product placement in a department or grocery store. Do you want your product or service to be somewhere in the back, out of sight, or front and center? A premium listing gives that to you.

ASK YOUR CLIENTS OR CUSTOMERS TO WRITE A REVIEW AND INCENTIVIZE IF NEEDED

Your clients or customers might be happy to write a positive review for your business, but they may need some coaxing first. That could come in the form of a gentle nudge—a friendly request—or with an incentive, such as a discount.

BrightLocal, a local citation platform, conducted a survey and found that 72 percent of customers asked to write a review did so.[9] This goes to show that simply encouraging customers to leave a review can make all the difference.

If you need to incentivize clients and customers to write a review (not just a "good" review either), try using product or service discounts or develop contests. Even better, partner with a charitable organization and donate a few dollars each time someone writes a review. People like knowing their efforts will help a worthwhile organization.

Two other types of incentives include monthly giveaways where you choose a reviewer at random and giving a small pre-paid incentive to everyone you invite to leave a review regardless of whether they do or not (it creates a feeling of reciprocity).

It can be difficult to get your customers or clients to leave you a review, so keep your ask specific and limited to one platform. Once you receive a review, asking them to simply copy and paste the same elsewhere is easier. In some cases, you'll be able to do it for them.

Whether you simply ask for reviews or pad it with incentives, always say a hearty thank you. For some customers or clients, that's reward enough.

Lori Strahlevitz, author of *Reputation Nation: Law in an Era of Ubiquitous Personal Information*, said that we now live in a world where various aspects of our conduct are evaluated often by anonymous individuals.[10]

For businesses, attracting new customers or clients and maintaining loyalty with their existing base means keeping a flow of uninterrupted communication with an optimized online presence.

Brands that encourage customers and clients to share their viewpoints not only empower people but also keep their businesses constantly improving. It develops a partnership between company and client that boosts your credibility, improves customer trust, provides a feedback loop between you and your customers, and rewards you with higher search engine rankings.

Regardless of your industry, make building and managing your business's online reputation a top priority. Remember, the real online currency is trust, and the more you can build with prospects, especially digitally, the more it will help transform your business and scale your new client/customer acquisition.

PART 4.

TAKE ACTION

FIND YOUR FREEDOM

The Big Idea: Success in life, sports, or business isn't about how many home runs you hit. It's about grinding every day and finding those small wins that add up to big things.

....

Starting a business and walking away from a paycheck is one of the most daunting and difficult things you can possibly do. I know what you're feeling: "it doesn't seem real, I can't absorb the risk, I need the paycheck/benefits/ stability." I've been there, I've done that. But if you have the entrepreneurial fire burning inside you, then you know something is off. You know what you want to do, but you're stuck doing what you're "supposed" to do.

I've played baseball for as long as I can remember, roughly thirty-five years to be exact between youth and adult baseball. In those thirty-five years I've hit only one home run ... my first at-bat. Thousands of at-bats across my entire life, and not another home run. Seems pretty crazy, and I've often thought about that over time. But there's something I've learned along the way in my life as a marketer and now, as a successful entrepreneur, that couldn't be more true.

Success in life, sports, or business isn't about how many home runs you hit. Sure they're great, sexy, a big splash, but they are few and far between. It's about hitting singles, doubles, and triples consistently. It's about grinding every day and finding those small wins that add up to big things. If you keep going to the plate trying to hit home runs, you're going to set yourself up to fail. Take the base hits, work toward something every day, and you're going to build a sustainable business.

There's a line in the movie *The Rookie*, about a washed-up baseball player making a comeback, where the main character's father says, "Your grandfather once told me it was okay to think about what you want to do until it's time to do what you were meant to do."

I've always loved that line because that one sentence can mean two different things depending on how you interpret it. In the movie, no indication is given, leaving the viewer to make their own interpretation.

What's your reaction? Is it that you must be realistic and forgo your dream to make ends meet? Or is it to go for your dreams?

It is my hope, having read this book, that you choose the latter: Go for your dreams and don't look back.

My goal in writing *Anti-Agency* was to provide some guidance for those of you willing to accept that challenge. To take away a bit of the uncertainty and show you a path forward. To motivate people like you, those with entrepreneurial mindsets, who are either reluctant to start or not quite ready to build a successful digital business using the same types of unconventional strategies and tactics I used when starting and growing Socialistics.

I tried to be transparent in sharing my journey (as difficult as that was for me) in the hope it would inspire you to take the leap of faith and scratch that entrepreneurial itch (and any other clichés I can think of that fit), to bravely chart a course toward a future and not surrender to fear. I also tried to educate you and give you actionable direction and practical tools you can use to build a million-dollar business of your own.

In part one, I shared the story of my entrepreneurial journey. Then, I advised you to follow my lead by starting your business with the runway approach—a side hustle—before going full time. I also encouraged you to be true to your values and tell your story authentically to earn prospective clients' trust.

In part two, I listed a series of business essentials—foundational items you need to put in place from the outset. I explained why you should start with a virtual office, hire a world-class team, build a back office, and set up a support system consisting of mentors, colleagues, and partners. I stressed the value of saying no to the wrong clients and strongly emphasized the need to empower your team.

The final section discussed ways to grow your business by walking the talk (show and not just tell), constructing a dependable pipeline to keep business flowing, finding the "big nobody" clients, rethinking cold email outreach, building your online reputation, and giving podcasting a try.

Did every piece of information and advice in this book originate with me? No. "There's nothing new under the sun," as they say. But what I have shared reflects my approach, which puts people over profits, compassion over commerce, and freedom over fear. Like me, I want you to become the person you always knew you were meant to be instead of accepting the "that's just what you do" nine-to-five mentality.

When you put this book down, go hit some singles. Then go hit some doubles. Then follow it up with some triples. Start small, build something on the side, and create some momentum for yourself, so you can take the leap like I did. It won't happen overnight, but take the first steps and work toward making it happen.

Like I said at the beginning, I'm just a regular guy who figured out a path forward in a way that worked for me. If any of the things I shared in this book have helped you figure out yours, then I did my job—and if that is the case, I would love to know. Reach out to us on social media or email me directly at jason@socialistics.com.

Still not convinced? Then go to https://www.jasonyormark.com/contact/ and book a free call with me and let's talk it through. I love my business, but I love helping aspiring or struggling entrepreneurs more.

Finally, if you would like to know more about me, visit my website www.jasonyormark.com. To learn more about my "anti-agency" company, go to www.socialistics.com.

Thank you for taking the time to read about my journey. I hope it inspires you to start yours.

EPILOGUE

My whole life I knew I was wired differently. I always felt compelled to be in charge, or at the very least be involved in the decision-making around the things I was associated with. For many of us, we're either born that way, or it's instilled in us at a very young age ... in most cases probably both. Even though I didn't always realize it growing up, or early in my career, I was destined to do my own thing. Every job I ever had was just a stop along the way to my inevitable destination of running my own business. If you're like me, you already know this, or at least feel it to a certain degree.

In the middle of my career, I was at a crossroads. I had thought that I wanted to be a teacher based on some of the early success I had being a high school girls' volleyball coach. Great plan, right? Good at coaching, so I would certainly make a great teacher, I buckled down and decided I would combine coaching, some side gigs, and pursuing a master's degree over the next few years. I thought it would be the perfect mix. Coaching a sport I loved, paired with the logical teaching gig, and perhaps a few side jobs to fill my marketing fix.

I powered through another two years of education. I was never a fan of school at any point in my life, so this was a struggle for me. I continued to keep my side business going, helping businesses with their websites and marketing to make ends meet. I never wavered on my plan, and it wasn't until I was thrown into student teaching assignments at the end of my master's program that I learned the painful truth: while coaching was a fantastic use of my skills and passion, teaching was definitely not.

Looking back, I realized that coaching was just another example of my love and passion of being a leader. Overseeing something and having the freedom to make choices without asking permission. While there are certainly parallels between coaching and teaching, those didn't really apply to me, and I struggled to find my fit in the classroom. I knew relatively quickly that I had made an error in judgment and that I was going to eventually need to pivot yet again in my career.

Luckily for me, those side jobs kept me in touch with a network of folks, and, as fate would have it, the digital landscape was booming. This was back in 2004, and a colleague of mine surfaced an opportunity with Microsoft.

They were hiring like crazy to compete with Google on search, and, at the time, Microsoft would have been on a very short list of companies I dreamed of working for, so, of course, I pursued. After a month or two of phone and eventual in-person interviews, I landed a job at Microsoft and packed my bags for Seattle for a new career and life.

For many people, scoring a job at one of the biggest companies in the world would be a finish line. While at the time that was what was in my head, little did I know that it was only another stop along the way. Of course, a very important stop as so much of what makes me the entrepreneur and business owner that I am came from my learnings and experiences at Microsoft.

Which is why, no matter where you are in your professional career, even if it's not where you want to be, it's likely preparing you for your inevitable path. If you've read this far, chances are that's starting your own business.

It's not easy, and it requires a tremendous amount of patience, dedication, and determination, but, if you're like me (and I bet you are), you'll take the tradeoffs any day over a traditional nine-to-five gig.

The best thing you can do is give yourself the time and preparation to chart your course. It's different for everyone, and only you can truly determine when the timing is right. But if you follow the steps I've laid out in this book and build yourself a runway, you'll find that, even if you are struggling in your current job, the sense of purpose in building something else for you to eventually jump into will make the steps along the way that much more bearable.

My life has never been better, and it all comes back to one word that hopefully has resonated with you throughout this book … FREEDOM. To me, nothing is more powerful than the freedom to live your life on your terms. No more commuting, no more unnecessary meetings, inefficiencies, workplace drama … you name it. The money can be great, but the time you get back in your life is priceless.

Start making your moves and work toward finding your freedom. You'll never look back.

REFERENCES

CHAPTER 4

1. Kim Parker, Juliana Menasce Horowitz, and Rachel Minkin, "How the Coronavirus Outbreak Has – and Hasn't – Changed the Way Americans Work," Pew Research Center, December 9, 2020, https://www.pewresearch.org/social-trends/2020/12/09/how-the-coronavirus-outbreak-has-and-hasnt-changed-the-way-americans-work/.

2. Enda Curran, "Work from Home to Lift Productivity by 5% in Post-Pandemic US," Bloomberg, April 22, 2021, https://www.bloomberg.com/news/articles/2021-04-22/yes-working-from-home-makes-you-more-productive-study-finds.

3. Julian Birkinshaw, Jordan Cohen, and Pawel Stach, "Research: Knowledge Workers Are More Productive from Home," Harvard Business Review, August 31, 2020, https://hbr.org/2020/08/research-knowledge-workers-are-more-productive-from-home.

4. Nicholas A. Bloom, James Liang, John Roberts, and Zhichun Jenny Ying, "Does Working from Home Work? Evidence from a Chinese Experiment," Stanford Graduate School of Business, Working Paper No. 3109, March 2013, https://www.gsb.stanford.edu/faculty-research/working-papers/does-working-home-work-evidence-chinese-experiment.

CHAPTER 9

1. Courtney Seiter, "What We Did after We Eliminated Performance Reviews at Our Startup," Fast Company, January 29, 2016, https://www.fastcompany.com/3056007/what-did-after-we-eliminated-performance-reviews-at-our-startup.

CHAPTER 14

1. Guillaume Cabane, "The 4 Rules for Sending Cold Email that Converts in 2018," Clearbit, January 30, 2018, https://clearbit.com/blog/the-4-rules-for-sending-cold-email-that-converts-in-2018/.

2. "What Are the Average Click and Read Rates for Email Campaigns?" Campaign Monitor, https://www.campaignmonitor.com/resources/knowledge-base/what-are-the-average-click-and-read-rates-for-email-campaigns/.

CHAPTER 15

1. "Online Reputation Management Statistics 2019," DigitalOx, November 16, 2020, https://www.digitalox.co.uk/online-reputation-management-statistics-2019/.

2. Kim Barloso, "Online Reviews Statistics You Should Know in 2021," Rize, April 28, 2021, https://rizereviews.com/online-reviews-statistics-you-should-know-in-2021/.

3. Ibid.

4. Felix Richer, "Facebook Reaches 3.2 Billion People Each Month," Statista, December 10, 2020, https://www.statista.com/chart/2183/facebooks-mobile-users/.

5. Ginny Mineo, "The Do's and Don'ts of How to Use Facebook for Business," HubSpot, https://blog.hubspot.com/marketing/dos-donts-facebook-business-infographic.

6. Statista Research Department, "Cumulative Number of Reviews Submitted to Yelp from 2009 to 2020," Statista, February 11, 2021, https://www.statista.com/statistics/278032/cumulative-number-of-reviews-submitted-to-yelp/.

7. Ibid.

8. Brittany Belt, "Study: 92% of Consumers Using Yelp Make a Purchase after Visiting the Platform," Yelp, May 22, 2017, https://blog.yelp.com/2017/05/study-92-consumers-using-yelp-make-purchase-visiting-platform.

9. Rosie Murphy, "Local Consumer Review Survey 2020," BrightLocal, December 9, 2020, https://www.brightlocal.com/research/local-consumer-review-survey/.

10. Lori J. Strahilevitz, "Reputation Nation: Law in an Era of Ubiquitous Personal Information," Northwestern University Law Review 102 (2008), https://papers.ssrn.com/sol3/papers.cfm?abstract_id=1028875.

CPSIA information can be obtained
at www.ICGtesting.com
Printed in the USA
LVHW111908220322
713946LV00011B/11/J